W9-DDJ-476

Halle Berry

Other books in the People in the News series:

Maya Angelou
Tyra Banks
Glenn Beck
David Beckham
Beyoncé
Sandra Bullock
Fidel Castro
Kelly Clarkson
Hillary Clinton
Miley Cyrus
Ellen Degeneres
Johnny Depp
Leonardo DiCaprio
Hilary Duff
Zac Efron
Brett Favre
50 Cent
Jeff Gordon
Al Gore
Tony Hawk
Salma Hayek
Jennifer Hudson
LeBron James
Jay-Z
Derek Jeter
Steve Jobs
Dwayne Johnson
Angelina Jolie
Jonas Brothers
Kim Jong II
Coretta Scott King

Ashton Kutcher
Spike Lee
George Lopez
Tobey Maguire
Eli Manning
John McCain
Barack Obama
Michelle Obama
Apolo Anton Ohno
Danica Patrick
Nancy Pelosi
Katy Perry
Tyler Perry
Queen Latifah
Daniel Radcliffe
Condoleezza Rice
Rihanna
Alex Rodriguez
Derrick Rose
J.K. Rowling
Shakira
Tupac Shakur
Will Smith
Gwen Stefani
Ben Stiller
Hilary Swank
Justin Timberlake
Usher
Denzel Washington
Serena Williams
Oprah Winfrey

Halle Berry

By: Michael V. Uschan

LUCENT BOOKS
A part of Gale, Cengage Learning

GALE
CENGAGE Learning·

Detroit • New York • San Francisco • New Haven, Conn • Waterville, Maine • London

LIBRARY OF CONGRESS CATALOGING-IN-PUBLICATION DATA

Uschan, Michael V., 1948-
  Halle Berry / By Michael V. Uschan.
    p. cm. -- (People in the news)
  Includes bibliographical references and index.
  ISBN 978-1-4205-0817-8 (hardcover)
  1. Berry, Halle--Juvenile literature. 2. Motion picture actors and
actresses--United States--Biography--Juvenile literature. 3. African American
motion picture actors and actresses--Biography--Juvenile literature. I. Title.
  PN2287.B4377U83 2012
  791.4302'8092--dc23
  [B]
                                                              2011052302

Lucent Books
27500 Drake Rd
Farmington Hills MI 48331

ISBN-13: 978-1-4205-0817-8
ISBN-10: 1-4205-0817-2

Printed in the United States of America
2 3 4 5 6 7 16 15 14 13 12

Contents

Fame and celebrity are alluring. People are drawn to those who walk in fame's spotlight, whether they are known for great accomplishments or for notorious deeds. The lives of the famous pique public interest and attract attention, perhaps because their experiences seem in some ways so different from, yet in other ways so similar to, our own.

Newspapers, magazines, and television regularly capitalize on this fascination with celebrity by running profiles of famous people. For example, television programs such as *Entertainment Tonight* devote all their programming to stories about entertainment and entertainers. Magazines such as *People* fill their pages with stories of the private lives of famous people. Even newspapers, newsmagazines, and television news frequently delve into the lives of well-known personalities. Despite the number of articles and programs, few provide more than a superficial glimpse at their subjects.

Lucent's People in the News series offers young readers a deeper look into the lives of today's newsmakers, the influences that have shaped them, and the impact they have had in their fields of endeavor and on other people's lives. The subjects of the series hail from many disciplines and walks of life. They include authors, musicians, athletes, political leaders, entertainers, entrepreneurs, and others who have made a mark on modern life and who, in many cases, will continue to do so for years to come.

These biographies are more than factual chronicles. Each book emphasizes the contributions, accomplishments, or deeds that have brought fame or notoriety to the individual and shows how that person has influenced modern life. Authors portray their subjects in a realistic, unsentimental light. For example, Bill Gates—cofounder of the software giant Microsoft—has been instrumental in making personal computers the most vital tool of the modern age. Few dispute his business savvy, his perseverance, or his technical expertise, yet critics say he is ruthless in his dealings with competitors and driven more by his desire to maintain Microsoft's dominance in the computer industry than by an interest in furthering technology.

In these books, young readers will encounter inspiring stories about real people who achieved success despite enormous obstacles. Oprah Winfrey—one of the most powerful, most watched, and wealthiest women in television history—spent the first six years of her life in the care of her grandparents while her unwed mother sought work and a better life elsewhere. Her adolescence was colored by pregnancy at age fourteen, rape, and sexual abuse.

Each author documents and supports his or her work with an array of primary and secondary source quotations taken from diaries, letters, speeches, and interviews. All quotes are footnoted to show readers exactly how and where biographers derive their information and provide guidance for further research. The quotations enliven the text by giving readers eyewitness views of the life and accomplishments of each person covered in the People in the News series.

In addition, each book in the series includes photographs, annotated bibliographies, timelines, and comprehensive indexes. For both the casual reader and the student researcher, the People in the News series offers insight into the lives of today's newsmakers—people who shape the way we live, work, and play in the modern age.

Actress, History Maker, Barrier Breaker

Halle Berry first made *People* magazine's "50 Most Beautiful People" list in 1992, after the twenty-three-year-old actress started becoming famous for her performance as a crack addict in director Spike Lee's movie *Jungle Fever* and her starring role in the television miniseries *Queen*. Since then the former beauty queen—she won the titles of Miss Teen All-American in 1985 and Miss Ohio USA in 1986—has appeared on many other lists of the world's most beautiful women. Berry has also been featured in advertisements for Revlon cosmetics, and in 2011 she launched her own celebrity perfume, Reveal. In its March 2011 edition *Ebony* magazine published "Hottest in Hollywood," a two-page spread of photographs of African American actresses attending the Academy Awards ceremony a month earlier. The biggest picture is one of Berry in a simple, yet elegant black gown. The caption accompanying the photo raves about how beautiful Berry still is more than two decades after *People* anointed her as one of the world's most beautiful women: "She does breathtaking better than anyone in show business. She is classic and sexy [and] 44 [years old] never looked so good."[1]

The compliment is one any mature actress should love. But in an insightful interview just a few pages later in the magazine's feature story—her picture also graces the cover of the issue—Berry

Halle Berry has been awarded one of People magazine's "Most Beautiful People". Berry doesn't want her beauty to define her, and has sought controversial acting roles to break these social stereotypes.

explains that she has always hated that the first thing most people mention about her is how she looks. When asked if "beauty is a burden," Berry responded,

> No, I mean, beauty is subjective. [And] there are worse things people could say about me. I do wish people would notice other things *about* me. I wish people would talk more about my talent than they do my beauty. I've worked really hard as an actress and I always try to push the envelope, grow and do something different. And I wish people would maybe notice more than that which I have no control over, which is how I look.[2]

Berry has always worried that her beauty defines her in the eyes of the public. To prove that she is much more than a pretty face, Berry has taken on many diverse, difficult, and sometimes controversial acting roles. By doing so she has broken racial barriers and made Hollywood history.

A Lesson in Racism

Berry is biracial; her mom was a white woman from England and her father was African American. Berry grew up in Oakwood Village, a white suburb of Cleveland, Ohio, and her light brown skin and mixed-race features led some white children to mockingly call her "Oreo" and "zebra." Such racist taunts forced Berry to confront her racial identity at an early age. Berry says the racism she encountered as a child made her will herself to overcome any preconceptions people might have if they tried to judge her only by her skin color and the way she looked. In an interview, Berry said,

> Society has labeled me as black. I have chosen to accept that. If you are black, you can't compromise or lose that. You are black every second, every minute, every day. If I could take my blackness off and be white for a day, that would be compromising it. I was told as a kid: "In order for you to fight racism and discrimination, you have to be better. Then you cannot be denied.[3]

Berry's drive to prove that she could be as good as anyone and to fight racism has led her to accept challenging roles that dealt with race. In 1999 Berry played the title role in *Introducing Dorothy Dandridge*, a television movie about a black actress and singer whose career in the 1950s and 1960s was negatively affected by racism, and in 2001 she starred in *Monster's Ball*, a movie that dealt with the harsh realities of racism. She won the Golden Globe Award for Best Performance by an Actress in a Motion Picture (Drama) for her role as Dandridge, and she won the Academy Award for Best Actress for her dramatic portrayal of Leticia Musgrove in *Monster's Ball*. She was the first African American in the history of the Academy Awards to win the best actress award.

Berry has also broken racial barriers in movies by playing parts that would typically have gone to white actresses. In 2004 she starred in *Catwoman*, playing a superhero who had mostly been played by Caucasians. Berry also portrayed Frost in several *X-Men* movies, although Frost is African American. Berry is the only black actress to star as two different comic book superheroes. Her beauty and acting ability also earned Berry a role in the 2002 James Bond movie *Die Another Day*. In previous movies about the British secret agent, the beautiful, sexy female heroines and villainesses who became known as "Bond girls" had almost always been played by white actresses.

In addition to becoming a "Bond girl," Berry also created a character that was the opposite of the weak beauties who Bond encountered in previous movies. Instead, Berry played Jinx, a tough, competent secret agent who was a worthy partner to Bond in fighting the movie's villain. Berry describes the relationship between her character and the macho Bond: "All their verbal exchanges are as equals, and so are their love scenes. This time there was a definite effort to make James more vulnerable and the women characters less vulnerable."[4]

Jinx was the perfect role for Berry, who was accustomed to acting against type and fighting to make people realize she was more than just a beautiful woman. In a 2007 interview Berry explained that being strong and defying stereotypes was integral to the path she had chosen as an actress: "For me, for the last

20 years, as a woman of color I've been having to make a way out of no way. I've been trying to make my way as a black woman my whole life. And I've been able to make a way. It's been tough, but I'm used to the fight. I will fight the fight and find a way. I've been doing it my whole career."[5]

Chapter 1

Growing up Biracial

Halle Berry is one of the most beautiful women in the world and an extremely popular movie star. While she is confident and successful, Berry is mindful of the struggles she experienced early in life. Berry once said in an interview that as a child she lived in fear and had a poor self-image because of a violent home life and racism: "I think I've spent my adult life dealing with the sense of low self-esteem that [such experiences] sort of implanted in me. Somehow I felt not worthy. Before I'm 'Halle Berry,' I'm little Halle … a little girl growing [up] in this environment that damaged me. I've spent my adult life trying to really heal from that."[6]

Berry gave that answer when a reporter asked why she volunteers in Los Angeles, California, at the Jenesse Center, a shelter that helps women escape from abusive relationships. She helps out at the center because of her personal experience—a father who abused family members when he drank.

A Violent Home

Berry was born on August 14, 1966, at Cleveland City Hospital in Cleveland, Ohio. She was born Maria Halle Berry, but in 1971 her mother legally changed her name to Halle Berry because Halle liked her middle name better. Berry's unusual name comes from an unusual source—a department store. Berry explains how her mom decided to name her Halle: "My mother was shopping in Halle Brothers in Cleveland. She saw their bags and thought, 'That's what I'm going to name my child.' No one ever says it right. It's *Halle*, like *Sally*."[7]

Halle Berry is an active supporter of the Jenesse Center, a center that helps women escape from abusive relationships, because of her own memories of her father's abusive treatment toward her mother. She has volunteered and participated in charity events, such as the Jenesse Center's Silver Rose Gala, to show her support.

Berry's mother, Judith Ann Hawkins, was a psychiatric nurse. She was born in Liverpool, England, and moved to Ohio when she was ten years old. Halle's father, Jerome Jesse Berry, was an African American hospital attendant, who worked in the same psychiatric ward as Judith. They married even though Judith's family objected to their daughter marrying a black man. The couple had two children together; Berry's sister, Heidi, is four years older than she is.

Judith remembers her husband as a kind, loving man except when he drank. When he did, he sometimes beat his wife and older daughter. One of Berry's earliest memories is of her father throwing the family pet, a tiny Maltese terrier, against a wall and of the blood that flowed from the dog's mouth because it had bitten its tongue. Berry says that memory is the strongest one she has of her father: "When somebody mentions my father, that's

Berry and her mother, Judith Ann Hawkins, at the 2003 induction ceremony for her star on the Hollywood Walk of Fame. As a child, Halle Berry witnessed her mother's abuse for years, feeling helpless and scared. Berry often brings her mother to award ceremonies and other Hollywood-related events.

the first thing I think about—that dog flying across the room. I remember saying, 'God, let him leave!' so that my life could get back to normal."[8]

Berry's father never physically abused her, but the harm he did to her mother and sister left her with deep emotional scars. When her father started beating her mother, Heidi would sometimes try to protect her, only to be beaten as well. Berry claims that the worst part of the violence for her was that he "never abused me. I was dealing with a lot of guilt because I saw my sister go through terrible beatings. I felt helpless and like a coward because I didn't do anything and couldn't do anything."[9] Psychiatrists say such feelings are common among children of abusive parents.

Berry's home life improved after her parents divorced when she was four years old. But in 1975, when Berry was nine years old, Judith invited her ex-husband to live with them again because she thought her daughters needed a father figure. Berry says it was a mistake because he was still drinking: "He lived with us for one year and it was the worst year of my life."[10] Berry's father left again and never returned.

Judith then tried something else to improve the lives of her daughters: She moved them out of the black neighborhood in Cleveland where they had been living. In an attempt to give her children a chance at a better education and life, Judith moved herself and her daughters to Oakwood Village, a nearly all-white Cleveland suburb.

The Wrong Color

Judith's salary as a psychiatric nurse allowed her to buy a two-story brick home with a big lawn in Oakwood Village. In many ways the neighborhood was an ideal place to grow up in, but Berry encountered problems because of her race. Being biracial can be difficult because at times both blacks and whites will reject a biracial person. Berry told one reporter, "Early on I lived in a black neighborhood where I wasn't accepted because my mother was white. Then we moved to a white neighborhood where they didn't like me because I was black."[11]

"A Black Little Girl"

Halle Berry's white mother helped her come to terms at an early age with her biracial heritage. Judith Berry explained to her daughter that even though she only had one black parent, people would consider her black because of her light-brown skin. In the following excerpt from *Halle Berry: A Stormy Life* author Frank Sanello describes the conversation:

> One of Halle's earliest memories is of Judith sitting her down in front of a mirror and saying, "Look at yourself. What do you see when you look at your skin?" I said, "Brown." She asked, "What color do you see when you look at my skin?" I said, "White." She said, "That's right: you're black and I'm white, but that doesn't mean I'm not your mother, that I don't love you. You are a black little girl." Halle credits her mother with teaching her to identify herself as black because that's how everyone else would classify her based on her looks. Strangers wouldn't know she was bi-racial, Judith told her daughter, and they wouldn't care even if they knew. Halle says, "I'm discriminated against like a black woman, as if I were one hundred percent African American, so that's what I feel I am."

Frank Sanello. *Halle Berry: A Stormy Life*. London: Virgin Books, 2004, pp. 10–11.

Even though Judith was a single mother, she gave Berry all the love and encouragement the young girl needed. Berry says, "I had a very strong mother. She was a white woman raising two black kids all by herself."[12] Berry, however, remembers that having mixed-race children was not always easy for her mom. Judith would become angry when people would stare at her and Halle when they were out in public because they did not know if she was the little girl's mother. Berry experienced more direct forms of racism. When Berry was in the third grade, she said a fellow student cruelly told her that her mother "couldn't possibly be her mother because had I noticed that she was white and I wasn't."[13]

Yvonne Nichols Sims, an African American, was Berry's teacher when she began attending Heskett Middle School. Berry claims that Sims was a guardian angel who protected her because the teacher realized the young girl felt insecure as one of the school's few black students. Sims said she tried to help Berry with her racial identity: "'Where do I really fit in?' was challenging for her. I told her not to worry what anybody else thought, to be true to herself."[14] Sims was the first person besides her mother who helped Berry learn to deal with being biracial. Berry's mother had told her when she was little that people would always know she was black because her skin was darker than that of whites. It was an uncomfortable truth for a little girl to have to learn. But Berry says she has always accepted it because of the way she was treated as a child: "I remember my mother being very liberal and moral and teaching us at a young age about [being] interracial. I don't feel white, because I'm not treated like I'm white, and I feel the prejudices that go along with that. I [even] hated it when people came up to me when I was little saying, 'You're black, but you're not like the rest.'"[15]

Her realization of how the world would perceive her because of her skin color forced Berry to make a decision. She might be different, but she would work as hard as she could to be accepted.

Racism for the Prom Queen

Berry also encountered racism at Bedford High School. Hank Wojda, a childhood friend, says, "[At] Bedford High it was harder for Halle. She suffered through a lot because she was biracial."[16] Berry was one of only a few nonwhite students. To win acceptance and prove she was as good as anyone else, she participated in many activities. Berry was a cheerleader (her past experience in gymnastics helped her win a role on the cheerleading squad), editor of the school magazine, and a member of the honor society.

Berry once said that in high school "being as good as everybody wasn't enough. I had to be better. And that, in turn, made me very much an over-achiever."[17]

The racial chip on Berry's shoulder led to many achievements, but she continued to feel insecure about her position in a white school. Berry was initially rejected when she tried out for cheerleading because there had never been any black cheerleaders before. Yet she won a spot on the squad and was eventually elected captain. And even though Berry was a beautiful young woman, she worried, as many teenagers do, about how she

Successful But Not Happy

Halle Berry's experience at Bedford High School in Cleveland, Ohio, was filled with many achievements. And even though Berry joined many groups and engaged in a wide variety of activities outside the classroom, she never felt totally accepted at the nearly all-white school because of the color of her skin. In the book, *Introducing Halle Berry* by author John Farley Berry sums up her high school experience:

> Not everybody would agree that I was smart or funny or had a solid character. "Pretty" was said about me more than anything else. I got to the point where I loathed hearing it. I loathed being judged by my physical self. Because I knew that was the tiniest part of me. I couldn't take credit for it. I wasn't proud of it. Everyone comes in the package that they come in. I tried really hard to fit in. So I was in every club, the president of my class, in the Honor Society [but] I never felt equal. [I] could be president and head cheerleader, but they were white and I was black and I was different. I realized I always have to keep fighting.

Quoted in John Farley. *Introducing Halle Berry.* New York: Pocket Books, 2002: pp. 30–31.

looked. Classmate Amy Jorgenson claims, "Halle was gorgeous," but Halle always feared that her biracial features made her look strange to other students and Berry admits, "I was always trying to straighten my hair."[18] In high school Berry's hair was long and bushy, and she had trouble controlling it.

In 1993 when Berry was elected junior prom queen, she thought she had finally won acceptance from the entire school. That triumph, however, turned into a racial rebuff when her victory was challenged. Seventeen-year-old Berry had won by so many votes that some people claimed she must have cheated to win. To resolve the controversy, school officials suggested Berry share the title with the blonde runner-up as a compromise. Berry rejected that solution but agreed to a coin toss to determine the winner. She called "heads" and won. Berry says, "I felt like I was accepted there, until it came to being prom queen. It took me a long time to get over that."[19] She was further embittered when someone sent Oreo cookies to her home, a disparaging reference to her mixed parentage.

For Berry, the prom queen battle showed her again how many of her classmates and even school officials still harbored racist attitudes.

A Beauty Queen

When Berry was seventeen, her boyfriend sent her high school yearbook photograph to officials of the Miss Teen Ohio pageant. Three weeks later, Berry received a letter saying she had been chosen as a finalist in the contest. Berry had not known until then what her boyfriend had done, but she decided to enter the event. She won the title to advance to the 1985 Miss Teen All American pageant. Contestants were judged on how they looked in gowns and swimsuits and how well they presented themselves in interviews with judges. Berry dazzled the judges in all three categories to win the title.

In 1986 Berry won the Miss Ohio pageant and advanced to the national Miss USA pageant. In her interview as one of five finalists, Berry presented a positive message of what she hoped

In 1986, Berry was the first African American contestant in the Miss World Pageant. She finished fifth runner-up.

to accomplish if she won the title: "I would like to symbolize a very positive role model, not only for women, but for people of the United States. And through me, I hope that they could learn that no matter what race, color, religion or sex you are, you can be whatever it is you want to become."[20]

Berry's interview received the highest score of any finalist, but she finished runner-up to Christy Fichtner of Texas. Berry, however, was not quite done with beauty pageants. She entered the Miss World pageant. The event was held in London on November 13, 1986. The winner was Giselle Jeanne-Marie Laronde of Trinidad and Tobago, and Berry was the fifth runner-up. Years later Berry admitted that after the Miss World competition, she never wanted to be in another beauty contest: "I knew going in it I was all pageanted out."[21]

Like many young women, including former Alaska governor Sarah Palin, Berry had entered beauty pageants to win money to pay for college. Although some people feel such contests exploit women, Berry disagrees: "I spent a lot of time with a crown on my head. You're exploited if you allow yourself to be. Only good things came out of my pageant days."[22] A college degree, however, would not be one of them.

A Move to Chicago

After Berry graduated from high school in 1984, she worked at a department store and studied broadcast journalism at Cleveland's Cuyahoga Community College. The end of her pageant days, however, also meant the end of her college days because Berry decided to move to Chicago, Illinois, and become a model. She was pushed in that direction by Kay Mitchell, a Miss USA judge who was an agent for models in Chicago. Mitchell was impressed with Berry's poise and beauty and told her she would be successful as a model. Mitchell also told Berry she would represent her and help her get jobs.

Among Berry's first jobs were hand and lingerie modeling and appearing in catalogs for Land's End, Marshall Fields, and Lord & Taylor. Berry soon discovered it was harder to become a successful

Struggling as a Model

When Halle Berry moved to Chicago in 1987 to begin a modeling career, she was confident she would be successful. But Berry struggled financially as a model. Berry earned so little money that she had to share a small one-bedroom apartment with a dozen other young women who were also starting out as models. When living with so many people in such a small space became uncomfortable, Berry and another model pooled their money and rented an apartment by themselves. When her roommate unexpectedly left Chicago, Berry had trouble paying the thirteen hundred dollars in monthly rent for the apartment. Berry asked her mother for a loan but was surprised and hurt when her mom turned her down. Berry recalls, "I don't think she ever thought it would pan out. I said, 'Mum, I hate to ask you this, but could you send me some money or I can't eat this week.' And mum told me she wasn't going to encourage me to call home asking for money. I had to figure it out or come home. I was so mad we didn't speak for a year and a half."

While Berry was angry at her mother for not sending money, she admits that it taught her an important lesson: She had to be self-sufficient—and it made her a stronger person.

Quoted in Siobhan Synnot. "Berry Happy at Last." *Daily Mirror* (London), April 16, 2007.

model than Mitchell had told her it would be. One reason Berry had trouble finding work was that she was only 5 feet, 6 inches (1.7 meters) tall, short for a model. And jobs were scarce. Berry even had to travel to nearby Milwaukee to find work, and she often ran out of money. Berry says that to get free food "Me and my model friends hung out at a lot of happy hours eating [free] drumsticks."[23]

Vincent Cirrincione was a New York talent agent for actors and actresses. When someone sent him a picture of Berry, he was so impressed with her beauty that he contacted Berry and asked her if she was interested in an acting career. By this time Berry had been working as a model for several years. She had become bored with modeling and was considering a new career. Although Berry had never seriously thought about acting, she mailed Cirrincione a video from the Miss USA pageant. The talent agent was dazzled by Berry when he watched it: "I put [the video] into the machine, and she just lit up the screen."[24] He invited Berry to New York, told her he wanted to represent her, and claimed she could be successful as an actress.

After meeting with Cirrincione in New York, Berry went back to Chicago and pondered whether to leave modeling for acting. Three months later she moved to New York to begin her illustrious acting career.

A Survivor

Berry had the courage to quit modeling to try acting because she had become a strong person by overcoming the problems she faced while growing up. Berry once said of her childhood: "I did encounter violence and abuse as a child. It gave me an understanding of the damage it does and the inner strength you have to find to get through it [and] the will to survive and fight."[25] It also gave her the courage to try acting even though she knew almost nothing about that profession.

Chapter 2

Berry Becomes a Movie Actress

Vincent Cirrincione began helping Halle Berry find jobs when she moved to New York in 1989. At first the talent agent could only arrange work for her as a model. Berry, however, turned down such jobs because she was focused on becoming an actress. Refusing work hurt Berry so much financially that she ran out of rent money and had to live briefly in a homeless shelter. Berry once said she was willing to do anything at the time to pursue her dream: "I wasn't working for a while. I probably was about twenty-one. But a girl had to do what a girl had to do. You can do that when you're twenty-one and ambitious, and your eyes are this big and you don't want to go home."[26]

Cirrincione and his wife, Vera, helped Berry get used to living in New York. Vera even went with Berry on auditions, because she knew New York could be a dangerous place for a beautiful young woman. Despite her close relationship with Cirrincione, Berry did something that disappointed him: She cut her long hair without telling him. Cirrincione had arranged an audition for Berry for a commercial for NYNEX Corporation, a telephone company. When Berry showed up with the new hairdo, Cirrincione thought she had blown her chance for the job because long hair was the preferred hairstyle for models. He says, "I looked at that short crop and said, 'Well, there goes your commercial career.' And she said, 'That's not why I'm here.'"[27]

The short hair accented Berry's delicate facial features and expressive eyes. Berry said she cut her hair because other African

American actresses she was competing against for jobs also had long hair. Berry believed her new look would help her get noticed by people choosing actresses for commercials and television shows.

In the end, Berry proved wiser than Cirrincione. Just two weeks after cutting her hair, Berry won a role in a new television series.

Playing a Living Doll

In her first two months in New York, Berry failed to win roles in shows like *Days of Our Lives*, a daytime soap opera, and *Charlie's Angels 88*, an updated version of the 1970s hit series *Charlie's Angels*. The problem was that Berry had never done any acting; her only credentials were being a model and a beauty queen. Berry claims casting directors usually thought models and beauty queens were dumb and that their only talent was their beauty. She also believed her good looks hurt her at first because it was all people saw when she auditioned for parts: "I definitely understood the importance of my [beauty] very early on in my career and I knew I had to use it because it's one of my strengths! But at the same time, I also had to show I was capable of expressing emotion and that I was a complete actress."[28]

Her big opportunity came in early 1989 when she won the role of Emily Franklin in *Living Dolls*, an ABC television series about models. The show, a spin-off of the popular comedy series *Who's the Boss?*, centered on life at an agency for young models. Berry was glad to finally be an actress but unhappy because she said she was cast mostly because of her race to try and attract African American viewers. She even claimed that white writers mostly ignored her character because they did not know how to write for a black woman. As it turned out, Berry's chance to prove she could act was short-lived. Reviewers savaged the show, claiming the comedy was only funny unintentionally when the acting and plot were so bad that viewers laughed at the show itself. The show, which debuted in the fall of 1989, lasted only twelve episodes before it was canceled. It is only remembered for being Berry's acting debut.

Leah Remini, Alison Elliott, Halle Berry, and Deborah Tucker made up the cast of Living Dolls, *a spinoff from the hugely popular* Who's the Boss *series. Unfortunately, the series bombed, lasting only twelve episodes before cancellation.*

Unfortunately for Berry, her most memorable moment in her acting debut was one of the most frightening of her life. While taping one of the show's episodes, Berry fell into a coma and was rushed to a hospital. What doctors discovered would change her life forever.

Diabetes

Berry remained unconscious for seven days after collapsing on the set of the show. When she finally awakened, doctors gave her some frightening news: Type 1 diabetes had caused her coma. People who have diabetes can have dangerously high levels of blood sugar because their bodies do not naturally produce insulin,

Berry shares a tender moment with Barbara Davis, host of the "Carousel of Hope Ball" benefitting childhood diabetes. Berry collapsed on the set of Living Dolls, *leading to a life-altering diagnosis of Type 1 Diabetes.*

a hormone that regulates sugar levels, or because their bodies do not react normally to insulin. When a person's blood sugar is too high, he or she can become weak and pass out. Long-term effects of diabetes are even more dangerous, including possible blindness. Berry admits, "I was scared to death, I thought I was going to die."[29] Berry quickly calmed down when she learned that the disease is treatable.

Doctors told Berry she would have to take daily insulin shots to help control the disease. She would also have to monitor her blood sugar levels several times daily, a process that involves

Coping with Diabetes

In 1989 as Halle Berry was taping an episode of the television show *Living Dolls*, she began to feel weak and knew she had to lie down. But before she could, she collapsed. An ambulance rushed her to a hospital, and doctors determined that she was in a diabetic coma. In the following excerpt from an article by Bonnie Siegler in the *Daily Mail*, a London newspaper, Berry explains how surprised she was when she was told she had diabetes:

> Diabetes caught me completely off guard. None of my family had suffered from the illness and although I was slightly overweight in school, I thought I was pretty healthy. I fell ill—dramatically—when I was on the TV show, *Living Dolls*, in 1989. I felt I needed energy but I didn't even have a minute to pop out and get a chocolate bar. I didn't really know what was wrong. I thought I could tough it out, but I couldn't have been more wrong. One day, I simply passed out, and I didn't wake up for seven days, which is obviously very serious.

Quoted in Bonnie Siegler. "Halle Berry: My Battle with Diabetes." *Daily Mail* (London), December 14, 2005. www.dailymail.co.uk/health/article-371528/Halle-Berry-My-battle-diabetes.html.

pricking a finger so a drop of blood can be analyzed by a handheld meter. Berry also had to be careful about the types of foods she ate and how often she ate because both affect the blood sugar level. She was also advised to exercise regularly to control the disease. Berry accepted the medical verdict and became determined to do everything necessary to stay healthy: "When I found out I was diabetic, I took it very seriously right from the start and I realized it was something I had to fight. I know I'm not allowed to eat just anything I like and I have to treat my body properly."[30]

Being diagnosed with a life-threatening disease can often crush a person's spirits, but Berry claims that her diabetes had the opposite effect on her: "Diabetes turned out to be a gift. It gave me strength and toughness because I had to face reality, no matter how uncomfortable or painful it was."[31] Coupled with the shock of her new health problem, the failure of Berry's first television series could have been enough to discourage her from pursuing her acting dream. But Berry persevered and was soon rewarded with her first movie role.

A Spike Lee Movie

Despite its brief life, *Living Dolls* brought Berry to the attention of Spike Lee, the director of the 1989 hit *Do the Right Thing*, a film centered on racial tensions between whites and blacks living in a big city. Lee was now seeking black actors for *Jungle Fever*, a film about interracial romance. Lee himself was playing one of the leading roles and initially wanted to cast Berry as his character's wife. But Berry thought the part would be boring and asked for the role of Vivian, a crack addict. Lee hesitated to give Berry the role because she did not look like an addict. But as always, Berry was willing to fight to get what she wanted, and she argued with Lee for the more difficult, emotional role: "[Lee] said to me: 'You can't play this part because you don't look like someone who has suffered.' I said: 'What do you know?' and he replied, 'Well, you definitely don't look like you could be a drug addict,' and I said, 'What exactly does a drug addict look like to you?' I got the part!"[32]

Director Spike Lee and Berry on the set of Jungle Fever. *Berry had to convince Lee that she could accurately portray a drug addict, and ultimately Lee granted her the role.*

Berry had never associated with anyone who was an addict, so she needed to learn what the life of an addict was like. With the help of costar Samuel L. Jackson, who plays her husband, "Gator," in the movie, Berry met some addicts. Berry also tried to live the part while she filmed the movie: "I didn't shower, I didn't shave [my legs]. I went to a real crack den with an undercover police officer. These are things that today I doubt I would ever do, because it's too dangerous and it really doesn't make a lot of sense. But at that time, I was young and I was like, 'I don't know anything about crack. I've got to go see.'"[33]

In addition to not knowing anything about addiction, Berry also did not know much about acting. Her only acting experience had been in a Bedford High School drama class when she performed scenes from the play *The Effect of Gamma Rays on Man-in-the-Moon Marigolds*. Mary Ann Costa, Berry's high school drama teacher, claims that Berry had surprised her with the acting talent she showed: "She went into this other world. When you have the ability to create a character that well, you have to tap into something, somehow. Who knows where that came from."[34]

A Crack Addict

Halle Berry's role as Vivian in the 1991 film *Jungle Fever* proved she could act. The beautiful, elegant Berry transformed herself into a mean-looking, foul-mouthed addict, who became a prostitute to make money to buy crack cocaine. In her 2009 book, *Divas on Screen: Black Women in American Film*, film historian Mia Mask explains how important the role was in establishing Berry as an actress:

> The portrayal of Vivian remains one of Halle Berry's strongest performances because of the intensity she brought to the character. It marks a moment in her career when the performance was so strong that spectators could suspend belief, seeing only Vivian rather than Halle Berry playing a character. When [Vivian] first appears, she is seen at [her boyfriend] Gator's side on an outdoor basketball court late at night. Her eyes are wide, as if she's permanently startled; her movements are quick and jerky, as if she expects attackers to leap out from the shadows. Vivian and Gator launch into an obscenity-laced, drug-fueled argument that proceeds quickly and inaudibly. The indecipherability of their words suggests that they are a pair of doomed souls.

Mia Mask. *Divas on Screen: Black Women in American Film*. Chicago: University of Illinois Press, 2009, p. 206

An apparently innate ability to act helped Berry hold her own in a cast that included stars like Jackson, Wesley Snipes, Queen Latifah, Ossie Davis, and Ruby Dee. The movie was a hit and so was Berry. Film historian Mia Mask writes, "In the movie, she delivered a compelling performance."[35] The movie proved Berry could act and that she was not just another beauty queen seeking a career in movies.

"Queen" Berry

Berry's dramatic movie debut led to more movie roles. She appeared in two more 1991 movies, *The Last Boy Scout* and *Strictly Business*, and won a recurring role in *Knots Landing*, a prime-time television show. In 1992 Berry played a career woman who falls in love with a successful advertising executive (played by Eddie Murphy) in the comedy *Boomerang*, and she even appeared in a

Berry played sexy secretary Miss Stone in the 1994 movie **The Flintstones.** *The role was not written for a black woman, in fact, race was not taken into account when Berry was chosen to play Stone. Berry considered the fact that she was granted the role a triumph.*

music video for R. Kelly's seminal single "Honey Love." In *The Flintstones*, the 1994 live version of the famed television cartoon series, Berry plays Miss Stone, a sexy secretary.

Berry played the title character in the made-for-television movie Queen, *working alongside veteran actor Ossie Davis. This six-hour CBS television series gave Berry a lot of exposure, as she played a biracial woman dealing with racial struggles over thirty years.*

Berry is proud of her role in *The Flintstones* because race was not a factor in her being chosen. Berry's past experience with racism makes her sensitive to how people react to her, and for *The Flintstones* her race did not matter and she was thrilled: "I was the symbol of beauty [in the movie]—me, a black woman."[36] Her lifelong concern over racism also led her to accept the starring role in *Queen: The Story of an American Family*, a 1993 television miniseries about slavery.

Queen is based on a novel of the same name by Alex Haley and David Stevens. Queen was Haley's grandmother, who was born a slave but was freed by the Emancipation Proclamation. Queen's father was the white man who owned her mother, and Berry says the story is close to her heart because like Queen, she understands how it feels to be trapped between the white and black worlds: "Being interracial myself, it hit me harder because I realized that, had I been born a hundred years ago, this could be my story. Queen's life could have been my life. And that was horrifying."[37] The miniseries details the problems Queen encounters as a slave and then as a free woman in a racist society, including a period after the American Civil War when she pretends to be white.

The role was a huge opportunity for Berry to showcase her acting ability. As the star of the six-hour, three-part CBS miniseries, Berry is on-screen for most of film. Queen ages in the film from her teens to her late fifties, and Berry had to act in deeply emotional, sometimes troubling scenes that included being taunted by fellow slaves for being part white and, later, being raped by a white man. Queen was the first of many roles Berry would play in which she portrayed a strong female African American woman who battled racism. Her understanding of the character and dedication to the project won her praise from television critics, like Duane Dudek of the *Milwaukee Sentinel*: "Halle Berry gives a remarkable performance in the title role as the daughter of a slave owner and a slave. She conveys the naiveté; of a girl torn between her black and white roots and the cynicism of a woman rejected by both worlds."[38]

Queen eventually finds happiness by marrying Alec Haley, a widowed farmer. Their son, Simon, would become the father of author Alex Haley. Not long after Berry finished playing Queen, she also fell in love and got married.

Berry Gets Married

Despite a successful professional life, Berry's love life was a mess. By 1991, her string of failed romances, including one with actor Wesley Snipes, left her so depressed that she was crying almost constantly on the set of *Strictly Business*. Berry's attempts at finding love reached an all-time low when a man she was dating in the early 1990s beat her; he hit her so hard on the side of her head that he punctured her left eardrum, and she lost 80 percent of her hearing in that ear. Because of her own abusive father, Berry knew what to do: "I left so fast there were skid marks. It [physical abuse] never happened to me before—or since."[39] Berry has never identified the man but claims he is well-known to the public.

Berry and Atlanta Braves baseball player David Justice married in 1992 after a very public courtship. Berry met Justice after ending a physically abusive relationship where she lost 80% of her hearing in her left ear.

Several months after dumping her abuser, Berry, who was filming *Queen*, met with a reporter for an interview, and he said his friend, David Justice, a star outfielder for the Atlanta Braves, wanted her autograph. Berry had recently seen Justice on MTV's *Rock 'n' Jock* show and thought he was handsome and interesting, so she gave the reporter her telephone number along with the autograph. Justice called less than an hour later. They met after a Braves' game and began dating.

Berry says Justice was the first man she dated who became a good friend. She also thought that he was gentle, which was vitally important after her last relationship because "I didn't want to fear that he was going to hit me."[40] When they decided to get married, some people thought Berry was making a mistake, because getting married could hurt her career. But Berry was deeply in love and responded to those critics by saying, "People say, 'Oh, you're too young, and you have this great career.' But when you find that someone special, what's too young?"[41] Berry married Justice on December 21, 1992.

The Whole Package

Marriage did not slow Berry's career. After working with her on *The Flintstones*, director Brian Levant commented on how versatile Berry was as an actress: "The range she's capable of is phenomenal. She can go from good girl to vamp like you and I shed socks. So few people can do comedy and drama. But that's Halle—beautiful, funny, the entire package."[42] In the next few years, Berry would live up to that compliment by acting in a wide variety of films that would fully test her acting ability.

Chapter 3

Berry Becomes a Star

I t took Halle Berry only a few years from the time she debuted in *Living Dolls* in 1989 to establish herself as a talented actress who could handle many different types of roles. Unlike many African American actresses, Berry had even shown she was not limited to playing parts that reflected her racial makeup. Berry was praised for her roles as the crack addict Vivian in the movie *Jungle Fever* and as Queen in the television miniseries *Queen: The Story of an American Family*. She also won complimentary reviews as the race-neutral sexy secretary Sharon Stone in *The Flintstones*.

The variety of roles Berry was capable of acting reflected the biracial identity she had carved for herself from the time she was a child. Berry had always identified herself as a black woman because that is what people, black or white, thought when they saw her light-brown skin. But Berry had always fought to have people accept her for herself. For these reasons, Berry always seeks roles that reflect her entire persona. Berry once told a reporter, "I want to do roles written just for black women because that is very much who I am" but she has also stressed that "I don't want to be limited."[43]

Berry displayed her multifaceted talent by starring in *Losing Isaiah*, a 1995 movie about a recovering addict fighting to regain custody of her son.

Losing Isaiah

Although Berry grew up in a white Cleveland suburb with a white mother, she claims that her biracial heritage helps her understand the problems African Americans, especially women, face in a white-dominated society. This is one reason she was drawn to the part of Khaila Richards, a homeless drug addict. *Losing Isaiah*

Losing Isaiah was a gritty role that garnered Berry many rave reviews. The drama cast Berry alongside Jessica Lange, as two women fighting over custody of a small child.

begins with Richards breast-feeding her baby. She then puts her infant son in a box in a trash receptacle, places a board over it to protect him, and promises to return. Richards then leaves to get drugs. When Richards returns, the trash is gone. She frantically searches for her son only to have someone tell her that the police found a dead baby in the trash.

Richards's baby, however, is alive. Garbage workers saw the infant and took it to a hospital. A social worker, played by Jessica Lange, becomes attached to the baby, who has identification saying his name is Isaiah, and she and her husband adopt him.

Losing Isaiah

In the 1995 movie *Losing Isaiah*, Halle Berry plays a black woman seeking the return of her son after a white couple adopted him without her permission. The film touches on delicate issues, such as whether or not whites should adopt African American children and what rights, if any, poor blacks have to keep their children. Berry's background gives her a unique perspective on the issues in the movie. In the book, *Halle Berry: A Stormy Life* by Frank Sanello Berry comments on the problems interracial families encounter, including some she experienced as a child:

> Isaiah grows up in an all-white family and they treat him like he was just like they are. I mean that's lovely. But, when that child leaves that home, somebody's going to tell him, "You're black, you're different, and you're not equal to white people." I got the name calling [as a child]. I had a rough childhood. When enough little kids tell you that she can't possibly be your mother because she's white, and you're like six, what they say means a lot to you.

Quoted in Frank Sanello. *Halle Berry: A Stormy Life*. London: Virgin Books, 2004, p. 79.

Meanwhile, Richards is arrested for shoplifting, enters a rehabilitation program, and quits drugs. Three years later Richards learns from a social worker that Isaiah is alive. She and a lawyer, played by Samuel L. Jackson, then fight to get him back.

Berry has many dramatic scenes in the movie. In a confrontation with the social worker who adopted Richards's baby, Berry effectively displays the depth of Richards's love for the son she was unable to care for while addicted to drugs: "Oh, so you're calling me an animal? If you think you're just gonna walk up in this court and take my baby like you take some puppy from a pound, you got another thing coming, lady, 'cause you ain't gonna take my baby from me."[44]

Richards eventually wins custody of Isaiah, but soon realizes her son is so attached to the social worker that he could never be happy with her. In an act that shows how much she loves Isaiah, Richards returns the boy. Berry won rave reviews for her deeply moving performance as a young woman torn about what was best for her son. *New York Times* critic Janet Maslin writes, "Ms. Berry is the most gorgeous young actress in American films right now, and she tackles this role with impressive passion. When a performer can look like a beauty queen and persuade an audience to follow her anywhere, she's a real star."[45]

A Busy Year

In 1996 Berry had roles in four films: *Executive Decision*, the most memorable of the four; *B.A.P.S.*; *Race the Sun*; and *The Rich Man's Wife*. *Executive Decision* was the first film for which Berry earned $1 million; she was the first black actress to ever make that much for one movie. Berry plays a flight attendant on an airplane that is hijacked. The terrorists have a plan to fly the plane to Washington, D.C., where they will blow it up and release deadly nerve gas over the nation's capital.

The movie was a big budget thriller, starring Kurt Russell and Steven Seagal. It was a major hit, and Berry's second film to make more than $100 million; the first was *The Flintstones*.

Berry became a Revlon spokesperson in 1996. This was especially validating to someone like Berry who had been bullied and teased throughout her childhood about her biracial appearance.

Berry's heroic flight attendant, Jean, aids Russell's character in fighting the terrorists and helps him land the plane at the end of the movie. Berry says she enjoyed appearing in the action film: "This was fun. In *The Last Boy Scout* [a 1991 action movie], I was killed at the beginning of the picture. This time it was great to be one of the survivors."[46]

B.A.P.S. (Black American Princesses) is a comedy about two waitresses, played by Berry and Natalie Desselle-Reid, who do crazy things to earn enough money to open their dream business, a combination hair salon and restaurant. In *Race the Sun* Berry plays a high school teacher in Hawaii, who motivates under-achieving students to compete in a science contest to build a solar-powered car. The film is based on the true story of a teacher at Konawaena High School in Hawaii and was the first in which Berry received top billing in the movie's credits.

In *The Rich Man's Wife* Berry is the central character in a mystery with a complex plot, involving adultery, blackmail, and the murder of her character's husband. Berry had never been in a crime film and was excited to do new things as an actress. But Berry admits she worried about the responsibility of being the movie's best-known actor: "It's satisfying, but I'm also scared to death! I'd be lying if I said that I didn't feel pressure, but I know why I'm doing what I'm doing, and I'm really doing this because I love to act. And I love to be in front of the camera. It's what I get the most pleasure from."[47]

Also in 1996 Berry became a spokeswoman for Revlon beauty products. Her Revlon debut was in a sixty-second commercial broadcast during the 1996 Academy Awards. Becoming a symbol of beauty for the well-known company was satisfying for Berry since she had felt the sting of racism for her appearance in the past. Two years later, *People* magazine named Berry one of the world's "50 Most Beautiful People."

All the money Berry was making from her movies enabled her to fulfill her dream of buying a new house for her mother. It was a big house on the shore of Lake Erie in an exclusive neighborhood in Cleveland. Her mother said, "She's a wonderful daughter. She made a dream come true for me. I never expected to live in a place like this."[48]

At the time, Berry was sharing homes in Los Angeles and Atlanta, Georgia, with her husband. But while her career was flourishing, her marriage was disintegrating.

A Bitter Divorce

Berry and David Justice were madly in love when they met. Justice said, "It was love at first sight for me," and after they were married, he claimed, "I tell Halle, 'I thank God every day

Divorce Hurt

Halle Berry became so depressed when David Justice decided to divorce her in 1996 that she briefly considered suicide. In an article by Laura Randolph in the March 1997 issue of *Ebony* magazine, Berry discusses how powerfully the divorce affected her emotionally. Berry says the love and support she got from her mother and friends enabled her to get through the difficult period in her life:

> I was numb for probably two months. I was walking around in a daze. I didn't know how I was going to function. I would wake up in the middle of the night and think this is just a bad dream. I kept saying "No, this isn't really real. David's just on a road trip." When it first happened, everybody who loves me rushed to support me. Thank God I had them because when something like that happens, you need people to hold you up, and I mean literally hold you up, because everything I thought I knew—my strength, my self worth—was in question. I think once you really love someone, a little piece of you always will. So some part of me will love David until the day I die. That's just a fact.

Quoted in Laura Randolph. "Halle Berry Interview." *Ebony*, March 1997, p. 27.

for giving you to me.'"[49] They even got tattoos of each other's name: her name on his arm and his name on her backside. But in March 1996, slightly more than three years after they married, Berry released a statement that said they were getting divorced: "It is with sadness that I announce that Dave Justice and I have decided to end our marriage. I live a very public life, but this is a painful and private situation that I am not prepared to discuss."[50] Although Berry was the one who made the couple's split public, she later admitted that Justice had asked for the divorce.

The Atlanta Braves outfielder was in spring training at West Palm Beach, Florida, when their breakup became public. Justice says their marriage failed because their jobs kept them apart. While Berry was making movies in Hollywood and around the world, Justice was playing baseball in Atlanta and other cities across the nation. Justice said, "We were bicoastal and didn't get a chance to spend a lot of time together," and a friend of Berry's told a magazine, "David wanted a wife, and she was always off making movies."[51]

The divorce turned ugly when Berry claimed Justice had been unfaithful and that she had begun to fear he would physically abuse her. For his part, Justice accused Berry of using the news media to portray him as the villain in their failed marriage. Justice claimed Berry was able to do that because of her acting ability: "People have got to understand that this woman is an actress. She can cry at the drop of a dime [and] she knows that the public will rally around her."[52]

Berry, however, was deeply hurt and upset that Justice wanted to end their marriage. Years later, Berry admitted she was so emotionally distraught about the divorce that she made a half-hearted attempt to kill herself: "I felt totally worthless. I put myself in the car with the engine running in the garage of my home until I could smell the fumes. I thought about what other people would think about my marriage being over and did not want to face them. The only thing that stopped me from ending it all was how my mother could ever deal with my death."[53] The couple's divorce was finalized in July 1997. Berry's antidote to her misery was to throw herself into her work.

Bulworth Controversy

One of the films Berry did in the next few years was *Bulworth*, a high-profile project with actor Warren Beatty. The 1998 movie is about a U.S. senator who is seeking reelection and who falls in love with Berry's character, a rapper. Berry had fun playing the part and even sported dreadlocks for the role. The movie angered some blacks because of repeated use of the "N word," Senator Bulworth's hip-hop clothing and his rapping of some political speeches, and his bizarre advice to blacks about how they could improve their lives, including quitting drinking malt liquor.

Some blacks also criticized Berry for appearing in the movie. Berry, however, did not understand why African Americans were upset with the movie. She explained that the sometimes racially offensive comments and actions of the characters should not be taken seriously because it is satire which is mocking conventional racial attitudes. Said Berry: "I thought black people would applaud this movie. I was baffled. My response was, 'Lighten up and look at the message and don't get caught in the stereotypes.'"[54]

Berry and Dandridge

But Berry soon showed other blacks how passionate she was about black rights and the racism that they often face. She was not only the star, but also a producer of *Introducing Dorothy Dandridge*, a made-for-television movie about the real life of a pioneering black actress and singer. It aired on HBO on August 21, 1999. For several decades Dandridge was one of the most glamorous and successful black actresses in Hollywood, and in 1954 she was the first African American to be nominated for an Academy Award for Best Actress for the movie *Carmen Jones*. Yet Dandridge was also a tragic figure. Her career was limited by the racism of movie executives, and she died of an accidental drug overdose on September 8, 1965, at the age of forty-two. Some people, including Berry, believe Dandridge committed suicide, because she was heartbroken at how racism had affected her life.

An eighteen-year-old Berry had become fascinated with Dandridge when she saw *Carmen Jones* on television. Berry says,

Halle Berry portrays Dorothy Dandridge in her most famous role: Carmen Jones. It took seven years for Berry and her agent to land a contract for the story of Dorothy Dandridge, a black 1950s actress and singer who struggled with racism throughout her career.

"I was mesmerized by her poise and her charisma. I had never seen a black woman quite like that in a film. She was someone I could admire and aspire to be like."[55] Berry also noticed the many similarities in their lives. Like Berry, Dandridge was a light-skinned, African American beauty. An even more direct link was that they were born in the same Cleveland hospital. Berry, however, claims that the most powerful similarity between them is their careers: "[We were] two black women trying to make it in

Dorothy Dandridge

Dorothy Dandridge was born November 9, 1922, at Cleveland City Hospital, four decades before Halle Berry was born at the same hospital. Dandridge's success in movies and night-clubs inspired not only Berry but also other black actresses, like Nichelle Nichols, who starred in the *Star Trek* television series in the 1960s. Nichols made history herself on that show by kissing actor William Shatner in television's first interracial kiss. Nichols said of Dandridge, "She was our queen."[1]

Dorothy Dandridge inspired many African American actresses.

Dandridge, who was nominated for an Academy Award for her role in the movie *Carmen Jones*, presented a glamorous, elegant screen image in films that made average black women feel good. Ruth Jeffries was thrilled to watch *Carmen Jones* at a segregated Nashville, Tennessee, movie theater because Dandridge's character defied the stereotyped image of dumb, ugly black women that existed in other movies of that period: "I had never seen a black woman in this kind of role [a] major role in a movie shown in theaters around the country. She wasn't fat. She wasn't a [racist] model. I remember her reading her response to the [Academy Award] nomination in some magazine. She said, 'You don't know how much this means to me.' We felt that way too. Young, black adults thought she was great."[2]

1. Quoted in Janet Maslin. "Hollywood's Tryst with Dorothy Dandridge Inspires Real Love at Last." *New York Times*, June 19, 1997. www.nytimes.com/1997/06/19/movies/hollywood-s-tryst-with-dorothy-dandridge-inspires-real-love-at-last.html.

2. Quoted in Mia Mask. *Divas on Screen: Black Women in American Film.* Chicago: University of Illinois Press, p. 23.

an industry that doesn't make much of a place for people like us. Dorothy was trying to carve a niche for a black leading lady back in 1953, and I'm still trying to carve that same niche in 1999. We share that struggle."[56]

Berry decided to make a movie about Dandridge because she believes that Dandridge never got enough credit for breaking racial barriers for black actresses. However, other people also wanted to make a movie about Dandridge, and Berry and her agent, Vincent Cirrincione, had to compete with black stars like Whitney Houston to win the right to make the film. In all, it took Berry and Cirrincione seven years to finalize a deal to film Dandridge's life story. The wait was worth it.

A Golden Performance

To accurately portray Dandridge, Berry interviewed many of the star's surviving friends and associates. Berry says they all claimed that the key to Dandridge's personality was "you have to find a way to be sad on every day, in every scene, in every moment. And always try to hide the sadness. And you'll get the essence of who she was."[57] Dandridge's sadness came from racist treatment and the way white directors and agents manipulated her throughout her career.

Berry's research and the similarities she shared with Dandridge helped her fully understand the woman she was playing. She became even more attuned to Dandridge when she tried on one of her gowns and discovered, to her amazement, that it fit her perfectly. Berry's hard work enabled her to bring the actress to life on-screen. Her performance was so stunning that Berry won her first major acting awards, including an Emmy Award and a Golden Globe Award. The National Association for the Advancement of Colored People (NAACP) also honored her with an NAACP Image Award. Berry was pleased to win all the awards and honors. But on January 23, 2000, when Berry received her Golden Globe, she said she felt she shared it with Dandridge: "Tonight, as you honor me, whom you really honor is the eminent Dorothy Dandridge. She never got to stand here and be recognized by her peers, but because she lived, I am able to. Thank you so much."[58]

Berry celebrates backstage at the 57th Annual Golden Globe Awards after winning the Best Actress in a Mini-Series or Motion Picture Made for Television. Winning this award for Introducing Dorothy Dandridge *was exhilarating for Berry, as Dandridge had been a source of inspiration since childhood.*

The award-winning performance elevated Berry into the ranks of the world's top actresses. And unlike Dandridge, who was often limited to racially stereotyped roles in films like *Tarzan's Peril*, Berry would now be considered for a wider range of roles, many of which would have nothing to do with her race.

Chapter 4

Berry Makes Oscar History

alle Berry met Eric Benét, a rhythm-and-blues singer whose hit albums include *True to Myself* and *A Day in the Life*, in 1998. Benét claims they met by chance encounters while shopping: "We used to go to the same L.A. [Los Angeles] mall, and she'd often come up and say hi. From there, we just began hanging out, and before you know it, we were an item. Or make that 'she' was the item. I was just the guy that the press would refer to as 'Berry and her escort, an aspiring R&B singer.'"[59]

Berry says their relationship grew slowly from those casual meetings: "There weren't any sparks or that mad passionate attraction in the beginning. Then one day I turned to him and said, 'You know what? I think I love you.'"[60] The bitter end to Berry's marriage to David Justice had made her wary about marrying again. But Berry believed her second marriage would be different because Benét truly loved her. Berry was also excited about the marriage because it made her the stepmother of his nine-year-old daughter, India. Berry looked forward to being a mother: "People say to me 'Oh, she's so lucky to have you in her life.' Well, I'm the lucky one. India sees me as unstoppable and when I'm with her, I feel that. It is such an incredible, wonderful feeling."[61]

Eric Benét and Halle Berry's friendship transformed into a romantic relationship. During the aftermath of Berry's accident, Benét served as a caring and compassionate presence for Berry. They were secretly married a year later, in January 2001.

A Car Accident

The life of anyone, even a world famous movie star, can change in a split second. After socializing with a friend one night in February 2000, Halle Berry got in her Chevrolet Blazer to drive home. At 2:30 A.M., Berry was going through an intersection on Sunset Boulevard in West Hollywood when she collided with a car. Berry's head struck the dashboard of the Blazer, causing a deep gash in her forehead. Dazed from the injury and not sure what had happened, Berry drove to her home just two blocks away.

A short time later, boyfriend Eric Benét returned to the house they shared. Realizing Berry was badly injured, Benét took her to Cedars-Sinai Medical Center where doctors closed the wound on her forehead with twenty-two stitches. Hetal Raythatha, a twenty-seven-year-old real estate agent, was also in the hospital's emergency room being treated for a broken wrist suffered in an auto accident. Raythatha recognized the movie star, thinking, "Oh,

A tow truck takes away Berry's Chevrolet Blazer at the scene of an accident involving the actress and a twenty-seven-year-old real estate agent. Berry was later charged with leaving the scene of an accident.

that's Halle Berry walking by."[62] Raythatha learned several days later that it was Berry's vehicle that had struck her much smaller Pontiac Sunbird. The car burst into flames and first responders had to pull her from the twisted wreckage of the vehicle.

On March 31, Berry was charged with leaving the scene of an accident, a misdemeanor with a penalty of up to one year in county jail and a ten thousand dollar fine. Raythatha, who says Berry left her to die in a burning car, filed a lawsuit against Berry, claiming that she was negligent in the accident.

Surviving the Accident

In addition to her forehead injury, Berry suffered greatly both emotionally and psychologically from the accident. For one thing, Berry worried that the incident would ruin her reputation and hurt her career. Some news reports contained inaccuracies about the accident, and Raythatha accused her of being impaired by alcohol or drugs that night, even though there was no evidence of that. Many people believed Berry had knowingly fled the accident scene, but what the public did not know is that the blow to Berry's head almost knocked her out and that afterward she could not remember what happened; both medical effects are possible from a severe blow to the head. Berry admits she understands the public's reaction: "I know people find it hard to believe because I couldn't believe it, and it happened to me. I was filled with more whys and hows than anybody because I had to live through it and explain it. I would sit for hours and hours hoping and praying that something would jog my memory."[63]

Making the situation even worse was that Berry could not tell her side of the story. Her lawyers advised her not to speak publicly about the accident for her own protection. Anything she said could be use against her in a criminal or a civil case. Berry explains, "For nine months, on the advice of my lawyers, I couldn't speak to anyone or defend myself and I had to let the rumors swirl and listen to all the jokes."[64] As with many other celebrities who get into trouble, comedians ridiculed Berry's accident without knowing all the facts.

Berry Grows Stronger

Halle Berry's auto accident on February 23, 2000, made her life difficult for months because of the legal proceedings against her. Extensive, sometimes inaccurate news media coverage of the accident showed Berry the cruel side of being famous. In an interview with Laura Randolph Lancaster for *Ebony* magazine in August 2000, Berry talks about being strong in the aftermath of the accident:

> Sometimes I wonder just how strong I really am. And this accident put everything I had to the test. I had to ask myself, "What am I really made of?" I can say I'm a certain type of woman—a woman of integrity and faith—but when the chips are down, could I put my money where my mouth was? And I got to prove to myself that I could. That I am the woman that I say I am. [I] did the best I could given what happened to me, and I was woman enough to take responsibility for my physical actions even though I did not intentionally do it.

Quoted in Laura Randolph Lancaster, "Halle Berry: Interview." *Ebony*, August 2000, p. 55.

Berry was not formally charged for more than a month after the crash. Berry said she lived in fear the entire time that she might be charged with hit-and-run, a felony that carried a possible one-year jail sentence: "Those days of waiting to know my fate were just indescribable. I didn't eat. I didn't sleep. I just could not face life."[65] The stress was so great that the already slim Berry lost 15 pounds. Berry also felt abandoned by friends who thought she had done something wrong. As Berry later put it, "I got to see who loved me—not Halle Berry in Hollywood, but Halle Maria who grew up in Cleveland. I got to see who liked being around for the parties and the accolades and who was really invested in me."[66]

On May 10, Berry pleaded no contest to the misdemeanor charge of leaving the scene of an accident. She was fined $13,500; placed on probation for three years; and ordered to perform two hundred hours of community service. Three days earlier, Berry had settled the lawsuit filed by Raythatha for an undisclosed amount of money. The accident and resulting legal problems had been hard for Berry to endure. She would later say that Benét, more than anyone, helped her survive the ordeal: "As the weeks went by, I thought, 'Wow, he's still here.' And not just loving me. Loving me hard. He showed me when I was too weak to stand, he would hold me up. When I was too fragile to think, he'd help me figure it out. When I was too scared to face another day, he'd be my rock."[67]

To Berry, who always worried about being abandoned because her father, Benét seemed to be a knight in shining armor. His loyalty during this difficult period was one of the reasons Berry married him a year later. They were married in secret on January 24, 2001, on a beach in Santa Barbara, California. Berry announced their marriage on her website. While her marriage was bringing happiness and stability to Berry's personal life, her career was reaching new heights of success.

A Mutant Named Storm

After *Introducing Dorothy Dandridge*, Berry starred in *X-Men*, a fun, action-filled romp based on Marvel comic book characters. Berry plays Storm, a mutant who manipulates the weather to battle evil villains. It was a demanding role physically, and Berry enjoyed performing her own stunts: "I was a gymnast as a kid, so any time I get to try to stretch my physical limits I love it."[68]

Berry was not familiar with the character of Storm, with her silver hair and strange powers. She remedied that by reading comic books suggested by director Bryan Singer: "I read some that pertained to the way he [Singer] wanted Storm to be played."[69] Other stars in the movie include Patrick Stewart as Charles Xavier, who teaches mutants to use their powers for good; Hugh Jackman as Wolverine; and Ian McKellen as Magneto, the villain who wants mutants to rule the world.

Berry followed up her serious performance in Introducing Dorothy Dandridge *with the fun-filled* X-Men, *where she played the popular character Storm. The film grossed more than $296 million worldwide and was a commercial success.*

Although the movie seems frivolous compared to some of her other films, Berry believes it has an important message. In the film the U.S. government attempts to imprison mutants because they are different. Berry said the moral of the movie, that people with differences can live together peacefully, was important to her: "[The mutants are] struggling to find equality within a society of non-mutants who fear them out of ignorance. I love the theme of the film, which is accepting people for who and what they are. That felt really important to me, especially being a minority in this country [the United States]."[70]

The special-effects driven movie opened in U.S. theaters on July 14, 2000. It earned nearly $55 million the first weekend and eventually grossed more than $296 million worldwide. Storm is one of the movie's most popular characters and *X-Men* made Berry more famous than ever.

Movie Controversy

Berry enjoyed the action film so much that for her next film she chose *Swordfish*, a thriller involving spies trying to rob the U.S. government of $9.5 billion. Actor John Travolta plays a corrupt government agent who enlists a computer hacker, played by Hugh Jackman, to steal the funds electronically. Berry plays the agent's assistant, Ginger, who recruits the computer hacker and helps with other details of the electronic theft.

Berry was paid $2.5 million, the biggest salary she had received to date for one movie. She enjoyed working with Jackman and Travolta, two of the biggest male stars in the world. What Berry did not like were inaccurate news stories about her first topless

Berry's topless scene in Swordfish led to much speculation and criticism within the media circuits. At the 2001 MTV Movie Awards, Berry dared co-stars Hugh Jackman and John Travolta to lift their shirts as a comedic retort.

scene. In the scene Ginger is seated, reading a book. When the computer hacker approaches her, Ginger drops the book and fleetingly reveals bare breasts. Some stories said producers inserted the scene only to publicize the film, and other reports claimed Berry was paid extra money to appear naked; estimates of the sum varied from $250,000 to $1 million.

It was not money or publicity that led Berry to agree to do the scene. Berry said she did it because she wanted to get over the fear she had always had of the consequences of appearing naked in a movie: "I did it because I needed to do it. I needed to face a fear. [It] gave me a chance to face this thing called nudity that I was afraid of. [I] had to get over the hang-up of, 'What will people say about me, or what will they think about me, if I decide to bare myself?'"[71]

The movie opened on June 8, 2001, and despite its star-studded cast, it was not a hit. Berry's next movie would also contain a nude scene, but that movie would be critically acclaimed and Berry's performance would make movie history.

A Monster of a Movie

Monster's Ball is a controversial film dealing with racism and the strange way in which race can affect personal relationships between blacks and whites. The film's main character is Leticia Musgrove, a poor black waitress in Georgia whose husband is executed for murder. In a bizarre twist of fate, Leticia becomes romantically involved with a racist white prison guard who had helped carry out her husband's execution. The movie contains brutal scenes depicting violence and racism as well as a torrid nude love scene between Leticia and the prison guard.

Despite the controversial nature of the movie, Berry desperately wanted to play the part after she read the script. Racism had played a huge role in shaping Berry's life, and she believed the film could be important because it discussed the difficulties blacks and whites sometimes have in living together. But Berry's agent, Vincent Cirrincione, told her the script had been sent to her only as a courtesy to a top actress. He said producer

Monster's Ball *appealed to Berry because of the strong*
racial themes. However, the producer and director did
not feel Berry was suited for the role because of her
beauty. Much like with **Jungle Fever** *and Spike Lee, she*
successfully fought for the role.

Lee Daniels and director Marc Forster both thought she was too
beautiful and elegant for the role of a down-and-out waitress.

Berry's beauty had often forced her to fight for the roles she
wanted, like that of the crack addict in *Jungle Fever*. So Berry
contacted Daniels and Forster and waged a fierce battle for the
part. She boldly told Forster, "Who are you to tell me I'm too
beautiful for the role?"[72] Berry also argued that being beautiful
had not spared her from episodes of racism in her life, physical
abuse by a boyfriend, or being poor when she was struggling

as a model. Berry told him: "I think being a woman, especially a black woman, I can identify with her struggle against racism. Feeling the effects of that on my life, and like most women who have had ups and downs, highs and lows, who have struggled at certain times in my life to understand who I am, to make ends meet, to make my way."[73]

Berry's verbal assault won Forster over but making the movie was even harder than getting the part. The budget for the film was so slim that Berry worried the money would run out before it was finished. She thought the movie's message was so important that she agreed to a salary of only a hundred thousand dollars. The film was shot in Louisiana in just twenty-one days. Berry worked so many hours every day that all she did was act and go back to her motel room to sleep, a routine that she later said helped her to stay in character. The acting was also emotionally difficult, in one scene her character beats her son, and in another she has sex with her prison guard lover.

When filming ended, Berry was exhausted but claimed "I knew that something wonderful was happening."[74] Berry would soon be proven right.

A Historic Oscar

Monster's Ball was a surprise hit when it was released on November 11, 2001, and Berry and Billy Bob Thornton, who played the prison guard, were lavished with praise for their performances. Berry's acting was so powerful that respected film critic Roger Ebert wrote that while he watched the movie "I was thinking about her as deeply and urgently as about any movie character I can remember."[75]

So, too, were many prestigious organizations that handed out acting awards. Berry won several honors for her role as Leticia, including a Golden Globe Award. Eclipsing them all was the Academy Award for Best Actress that she won on March 24, 2002. She was the first African American woman to win the award. In an emotional acceptance speech, Berry said that she felt she shared the award with other black actresses who had made her career possible by fighting racism to make movies in the past:

Berry gave an impassioned acceptance speech when accepting the Best Actress Oscar in 2002, saying the moment was for "every nameless faceless woman of color that now has a chance".

A Historic Night

The 74th Academy Awards ceremony on March 24, 2002, was the biggest celebration of African American acting in Oscar history. Halle Berry became the first black recipient of the best actress award (for *Monster's Ball*) and Denzel Washington was only the second black man in the history of the awards to be named best actor (for *Training Day*). Sidney Poitier, who in 1963 was the first black man to win best actor (for *Lillies of the Field*), received an honorary Academy Award for his long, distinguished movie career, and Whoopi Goldberg, who won a best supporting actress award (for *Ghost*) in 1991, was the host of the televised show.

Best Actress winner Halle Berry and Best Actor winner Denzel Washington backstage at the 2002 Academy Awards. The night was momentous for black actors, with Washington and Berry receiving top honors in their respective categories.

The first black person to ever win any award was actress Hattie McDaniel in 1940 for her role as a slave in *Gone with the Wind*. But even on the night that McDaniel was named best supporting actress, she had to sit in a segregated area at the ceremony. Few black actors or actresses have won Oscars since then, something that many people—both black and white—claim is due to racism. In an April 2002 article in *Jet* magazine, Berry explains how important the 2002 ceremony was for African Americans:

It's such a great night. I never thought it'd be possible in my lifetime. Maybe [in the future] we'll be judged on merit and not skin color. This is not just about me, it's about those who fought before me and along with me and for those to come. Today that glass ceiling was broken wide open. Tonight means every woman of color should be hopeful.

Quoted in "Halle Berry, Denzel Washington Get Historic Wins at Oscars." *Jet*, April 8, 2002, p. 14.

"This moment is so much bigger than me. This moment is for Dorothy Dandridge, Lena Horne, Diahann Carroll [and] it's for every nameless faceless woman of color that now has a chance [for a similar honor] because this door tonight has been opened. Thank you. I'm so honored."[76] Berry had broken another racial barrier. Her life would never be the same again.

Chapter 5

Catwoman and Other New Roles

Even though Halle Berry was already regarded as a top-level actress, winning an Academy Award helped her win a wider variety of roles, which was important because she enjoyed playing different characters. Berry's next movie was *Die Another Day*, the twentieth installment in the popular series of movies about British spy James Bond. Berry said that after her role as the emotionally tortured Leticia, it was fun to play Giacinta "Jinx" Johnson, an American spy who helps Bond defeat the movie's villain: "That's the real joy of being able to do this [acting] if I can go from one [type of role] to the other. After this [*Die Another Day*] I can come back and do another character-driven dramatic piece or a comedy that I haven't really done before. That's the real joy for me. If I had to do the same thing that I'd done before, or the same character, I think I wouldn't be as happy."[77]

Berry soon discovered that winning an Academy Award could negatively impact her professional life. Because the award stamped her as a fine actress and not just a movie star, some movie critics claimed she should only act in serious, important movies and reject frivolous films, like *Die Another Day* and *X-Men*. Berry, however, refused to restrict herself only to movies her critics claimed were worthy of an Academy Award–winning actress. Said Berry:

It's a funny thing but sometimes an Oscar [Academy Award] doesn't expand your options but restricts them. What is Oscar-worthy material? Who is to say that today? I think that it's about doing things that we love. There are a lot of styles of film that I haven't done and would like to do. [I] don't want to be denied the chance of the experience because of some notion that it is not of sufficient status.[78]

A Black Bond Girl

In her first scene in *Die Another Day*, Berry walks out of the sea onto a beach wearing an orange bikini with a sheathed knife on her hip. The sexy scene duplicated one in *Dr. No* (1962), the first Bond film starring Sean Connery. The beautiful girl in *Dr. No* was blond actress Ursula Andress, and since then nearly all the "Bond girls"—the nickname for the beautiful women in Bond films, whether they are heroines or villainesses—had been white. Even though Berry would not make movie history as the first black Bond girl—that honor went to Trina Parks in the 1971 film *Diamonds Are Forever*—she was thrilled to get the part.

Berry during a fight scene in Die Another Day. *Berry was very pleased with the script, saying that this Bond girl was more Bond's equal than in previous Bond movies.*

Like many African American actresses, Berry believes movie producers never consider her for parts in some major movies because of her race. Berry claims that being biracial cost her several roles in movies, including the part of a forest ranger. Berry says that she auditioned for the part in 1996 only to have a producer tell her she could not have the role because in real life there were no black female forest rangers, a viewpoint she considered racist. So for Berry it was very satisfying to win the part of Bond's love interest, a role that usually went to white actresses. Berry playfully bragged about her coup to a British newspaper reporter, telling him "I'm a Bond girl. Go ahead and say it. Say it! Classic Bond babe! And that's great!"[79]

Brosnan Saves Berry

Die Another Day is the fourth and final film in which Pierce Brosnan plays James Bond. As a heroic secret agent, Brosnan was accustomed to saving the lives of the "Bond girls" who were cast in his films as his romantic partners. But while filming the 2002 movie, Brosnan himself actually saved Halle Berry from possibly choking to death. In a love scene between Brosnan and Berry's characters a fig became caught in Berry's throat, making it impossible for her to breathe. Brosnan slapped her on the back to free the fig. In an article by Briony Warden for *The Sun*, a newspaper in London, Berry explains what happened: "Pierce saved my life, he really did. It was during our sex scene together and I was trying to be way too sexy for my own good. Anyway, this fig got lodged in my throat and he thought really quickly, jumped up and hit it free. It jumped right across the room. That has to be my favorite moment in the film because otherwise I'd have died."

Quoted in Briony Warden. "Bond Saved Me from Choking to Death During Our Love Scene." *TheSun* (London), November 13, 2002, p. 28.

Jinx is not only Bond's love interest in *Die Another Day*, but she is also a fellow secret agent. After Bond escapes from a North Korean prison, he hunts down the North Korean jailer who tortured him and the English billionaire who betrayed him to the North Koreans while Bond was on a spy mission. Jinx helps him get his revenge. Jinx was one of few women in a Bond movie who was not just a sex symbol to be saved by Bond but an equal who fought by his side. That new status delighted Berry:

> I like Jinx. She's really strong, and I like the fact she's the next step in the evolution of the Bond woman. Year after year they've gotten a little stronger, a little smarter, and more equally, yoked with Bond, while still retaining their sexiness. Now they are Bond's intellectual equals and physical rivals—and Jinx is one more step in that evolution.[80]

Berry also got to test her athletic abilities with fight scenes, including one with swords, and in a key scene at the end of the film when Jinx helps Bond land a plane. Berry enjoyed the challenge of the action scenes that came with playing a tough heroine because "it excites me, doing things that people think I wouldn't do."[81] Film critic Simon Wheeler raved that "Halle Berry is fantastic as US agent Jinx."[82]

Die Another Day was released in the United States and Great Britain on November 20, 2002. It was a global hit as it earned $432 million worldwide, the sixth highest grossing film of 2002. Berry gave such a spirited, powerful, and sexy performance that producers of the Bond movies discussed starring her in movies based on her character, something that would have made her the first female to star in spy movies. Although that never happened, it showed that Berry's fame and star power were at an all-time high.

Berry's Personal Problems

During the filming of *Die Another Day*, Berry was having problems with her marriage. In interviews Berry gave when the Bond film opened, she admitted that her marriage was in trouble. There had

Berry Wants a Baby

Halle Berry's two divorces soured her on the idea of ever being married again. Despite that, Berry still wanted to become a mother. During her second marriage to Eric Benét, Berry had enjoyed being a stepmother to his daughter India so much that she decided she wanted to have a baby even if she was not married. In a 2005 article in *Jet* magazine, Berry explains her feelings and even sets a deadline for trying to become a mother—her 40th birthday:

Before throwing the opening pitch at a Montreal Expos game, Berry listens to the National Anthem with then-husband Eric Benét and stepdaughter India. Berry has said that she enjoyed being India's stepmother so much, she knew she needed to become a mother.

I am who I am. I've had this tumultuous road. I don't need to get married, but I do need a partner, because I'm a very, a person who likes to be in a relationship and be committed. I don't want to be all over the town…. [On age forty] That's my limit for myself. If there's no serious man, whoever I'm dating at the time, I'll say, "Hey, would you like to have a baby? I'll sign a paper that will say I won't ask you for one red cent, one thing."

Quoted in "Halle Berry Says She Wants a Baby and Reveals Her Plans to Get One." *Jet*, May 30, 2005, p. 56.

been reports for some time that husband Eric Benét had cheated on Berry and had been treated for sex addiction. However, Berry also said, "We are facing a crisis, which many married couples face. [We are] facing it together. We're very much united [and] I think we're going to be just fine."[83] Berry even admitted the marital problems had been going on since before she won her Academy Award for *Monster's Ball* in 2002.

Berry attempted to save her marriage by going to rehabilitation sessions with her husband to help him overcome his sex habit. She even attended meetings of Alanon, a program begun in tandem with Alcoholics Anonymous that helps people who have a loved one with an addiction. Berry told one journalist, "There's a saying in twelve-step programs: 'You're only as sick as your secrets.'"[84] Unfortunately, Benét kept denying he had a problem even after details of his infidelity became public.

In addition to being unfaithful to Berry, Benét was also having trouble coping with having a wife who was more famous and successful than he was. The rhythm-and-blues singer explained that when they first began dating, he felt strange because more people noticed her than him when they were in public: "It was weird at first. Here I was used to getting most of the attention [but] now I was dating a woman whose profile was ten times bigger."[85] Benét's negative feelings about being overshadowed by Berry increased as her fame and success continued to grow during their marriage.

In October 2003 Berry announced and she and her husband had separated because they needed time apart to evaluate their relationship. The separation eventually turned into a divorce, which was finalized in January 2005. Berry's second marriage was even shorter than her first, and Berry was critical of herself, placing much of the blame for both divorces on the poor choices she always seemed to make in choosing the men in her life: "I'd be so busy wanting guys to like me that I never wondered if I liked them. Then I'd realize, 'You're a jerk.'"[86]

When people read comments like that, they have trouble understanding why a famous, beautiful, wealthy movie star would be so needy in her relationships with men. Berry claims that the sense of abandonment she felt when her father left when she was a child is the reason why she had such emotions. It was also during the period in which her second marriage was falling apart that her father, Jerome Berry, died in January 2003. Berry never reconciled with him before his death.

During this stressful time in her life, Berry worked almost continuously. Her heightened fame from her Academy Award and the success of *Die Another Day* had movie producers begging her to act in their movies. Berry gleefully told one reporter that "the biggest change [since winning the Academy Award] is that I've got jobs now, like in advance. Before, when a movie was finishing, I'd be calling my manager to say, 'Oh my God, we've got to get another job.'"[87] One reason for Berry's previous insecurity was that black actresses often had trouble finding roles because most parts in movies were for whites. But Berry was in such demand by 2003 that British journalist John Braithwaite commented, "She has taken black women to a new level of acknowledgement in the mainly white film industry."[88]

A Busy Berry

Berry had so many movie offers that she had to reject some, including *Gigli*, a movie about two criminals who fall in love during a comical, botched kidnapping. Berry had agreed to do the film but had to cancel her contract because it conflicted with the shooting of the second X-Men movie. Singer and actress Jennifer Lopez took her place, starring alongside Ben Affleck. Berry's decision was a smart one; most critics claimed *Gigli* was the worst movie of 2003, while *X2: X-Men United* was a smash hit, earning nearly $215 million in the United States and another $193 million in other countries.

Berry also starred in *X-Men: The Last Stand*, which opened May 24, 2006. The third X-Men film was an even bigger hit, earning nearly $103 million in its opening weekend to set a Memorial Day weekend record. Neither movie tested Berry's acting ability much, but she had fun starring in the smash hits. She was also drawn to them because of their messages that humans should not discriminate against mutants, because they are different. In the third movie the mutants are told there is a cure that can make

Not Just a "Black" Actress

Halle Berry has always resented that movie executives, most of whom are white, often refuse to consider her for roles because of the color of her skin. One incident that especially angered her happened in 1996 when Berry said a white producer told her she could not play the part of a forest ranger because there were not black rangers in real life. According to Berry, the producer made that claim even though he had no evidence to back it up, and she believes she lost the role due to racism. In an article by Nui Te Koha in the *Herald Sun*, a newspaper in Melbourne, Australia, Berry said, "To be told that you can't even audition for a part because somebody believes there are no blacks who actually do, or could do, that job—that is racism to the 100th degree. It's worse than being called a n*****, because it's saying black people can't do what the rest of us can. Because this man never saw a black forest ranger, in his mind, there were none. That is really, really scary."

Quoted in Nui Te Koha, "Down a Dark Halle." *Herald Sun* (Melbourne, Australia), March 23, 2002.

them normal. Berry said the plot made her think about the racial discrimination she had faced during her life and whether she would ever accept a "cure" to change her skin color:

I think it [the movie's story line] hit home with me being a person of color. If I could change my skin color and not deal with being different that way, would I? No, I wouldn't. But if a cure were to be devised and someone else wanted to take it, would I be opposed to them taking it? No I wouldn't. I'd love that we would have a choice [but] I'm certainly not one who would be in favor.[89]

Berry played another superhero in the 2004 film *Catwoman*, a spin-off from the Batman movie franchise. Berry was the second

Even though she looked great in the leather catsuits, Berry's movie Catwoman bombed at the box office. She received a Razzie Award for the Worst Actress of the Year. Berry actually showed up at the ceremony to collect the award.

black to play the role—Eartha Kitt was a seductive Catwoman in the 1960s television show *Batman*—but she was the first to play Catwoman as a hero instead of a villainess. The movie had been expected to be a big hit because of Berry's star power and the popularity of superhero films. Instead, *Catwoman* was a flop. Movie critics criticized the plot and complained that Berry did nothing but try to look sexy in tight-fitting, revealing, leather outfits. Critic Ann Hornaday caustically commented that "after her dramatic, toned-down turn in 'Monster's Ball,' it's as if she wants to remind audiences (and the powers that be in Hollywood) that she's really just a pretty face."[90]

Oprah Winfrey and Berry celebrate at the **Their Eyes Were Watching God** *Los Angeles premiere after-party. Winfrey's production company made the film, based on the best-selling book, and Berry starred.*

Many other reviews were equally insulting, and the Golden Raspberry Award Foundation, which jokingly gives awards to the year's worst movies and performances, awarded Berry a worst actress Razzie Award. Unlike most Razzie winners, Berry accepted hers in person at the group's annual awards show. She even displays it in her home with her other awards and brags, "My Oscar is also there. I am the only person to have a full set. It just reminds me of the absurdity of this career."[91] Despite the movie's negative reception, Berry claimed she enjoyed making *Catwoman* and thought the film was a good one.

Berry's next film choice turned out much better as she found the perfect role for her talents in *Their Eyes Were Watching God*. The film is based on the 1937 novel of the same name by Zora Neale Hurston, one of the early twentieth century's most celebrated African American writers. The novel tells the story of Janie Crawford's search for true love and spirituality. In three marriages, the young black heroine struggles to be an independent woman in a racist white society while also seeking true love. The story captivated Berry, who like Janie had failed to find true love in her own life. Berry said, "I think she was struggling to live and discover who she really was. [She] was struggling to understand why she was in this world. And I think that's a theme that I think people will struggle with until the end of time. We're always going to be searching for love. Without love, we don't have a life. There's no reason to be here."[92]

Harpo Productions, talk-show host Oprah Winfrey's production company, made the film for television. It was broadcast on March 6, 2005, and Berry's performance garnered rave reviews and Emmy and Golden Globe nominations for best actress. Despite failing to win either award, Berry showed the world once again she was a superb actress.

Berry Wants More

When Berry completed the third X-Men movie in 2006, she seemed to have it all—fame, fortune, and acknowledgment by her peers that she was a brilliant actress. She lived in an $8 million home on the beach in Malibu, California, and had moved her mother, Judith, to California to be closer to her.

But despite all that she had, Berry felt unfulfilled. In an interview in May 2006, Berry said she needed "a deeper meaning to get up in the morning. What feels important as I get older is that I need something more than a career. However that will manifest I don't know."[93] By 2007 Berry had discovered what she needed to make her life complete. In another interview, she stated, "I definitely want children."[94]

Within a year, Berry would realize her dream of becoming a mother. But even that joy would come with heartbreak as yet another romantic relationship would disintegrate.

Chapter 6

A New Starring Role: Motherhood

Halle Berry was thirty-eight years old in January 2005, when she divorced Eric Benét. The failure of her second marriage upset her, because she had a deep need to have someone in her life to love. So even though Berry decided, at the time, that she would never marry again, she kept searching for someone to love. In an interview, she said, "No more marriage for me. I've done it twice and I've failed. I've tried it so you can't say I don't know what I'm talking about. It doesn't work for me. But I want a committed relationship. I'm a relationship-oriented person. I'm just going to redefine that relationship, I'm going to redefine it for myself and it won't be a legal document."[95]

In November 2005 Berry began a long-term relationship with Gabriel Aubry, a male model who appeared in advertisements for fashion giants like Versace, Calvin Klein, and DKNY. Berry usually dated African American men, but Aubry was a blond, green-eyed Caucasian born in Montreal, Quebec, Canada. Berry and Aubry met while they were both posing for pictures for a Versace advertisement. Because of her past failed relationships, Berry was hesitant at first about discussing Aubry with the news media. But in early 2007, Berry briefly talked about him to a reporter: "I do have someone in my life who is putting a sparkle in my eye and he is ten years younger. I am not a girl who has had the best relationships so I don't really want to talk about it—my history will tell you why."[96]

Gabriel Aubry, a male model, met Berry at an advertising photo shoot and a romantic relationship developed. This relationship also granted Berry the child she desperately wanted.

Berry and Aubry began living together in her Los Angeles home as well as one near Montreal in Canada. Berry kept her vow not to marry again but the relationship allowed Berry to fulfill her dream of becoming a mother.

Nahla

Berry's new romance and desire to have a child did not stop her from working. Her next film after the third X-Men movie was *Things We Lost in the Fire*, a 2008 drama about how people handle grief. Berry plays Audrey, a mother of two whose husband suddenly dies. She and her husband's oldest friend, played by Benicio Del Toro, help each other cope with his death. Berry also helps Del Toro's character recover from an addiction to heroin. Both stars were highly praised when the movie opened on February 2, 2008, Del Toro for his portrayal of an anguished addict and Berry for her sensitive performance in coping with her

In 2008, Berry starred in Things We Lost in the Fire, *a movie about a mother raising her two children alone after her husband's sudden death. Berry's experience filming with the child actors added to her increasing desire for motherhood.*

own grief. Film critic Claudia Puig writes, "Berry's raw portrayal recalls her Oscar-winning role in *Monster's Ball.*"[97]

Part of the movie focused on Audrey's relationship with her ten-year-old daughter and six-year-old son. For Berry, one of the joys of being married to Eric Benét had been mothering his daughter India. The experience was so gratifying that it was one of the reasons she decided that she wanted a child. Berry's emotional scenes in *Things We Lost in the Fire* with the child actors strengthened her desire to be a mother even more. In an interview with talk-show host Oprah Winfrey on October 2, 2007, Berry said, "I think it validated that I was meant to be a mother, because every day I dealt with the character as a mother and thinking as a mother—and not having any children, that was a big leap for me. I haven't really played a mother, a loving, caring mother like this woman was. So it let me know that I must be a mother."[98]

"Halle Blueberries"

Halle Berry loves being a mom, but like any mother, Berry worries about her child all the time. And when little Nahla disappeared briefly when they were in a store, Berry had the same brief moment of terror any mother would in the same situation. In an article by Jonathan Van Meter for *Vogue* magazine, Berry explains the incident:

I took her [Nahla] shopping, and I had that moment that every parent has. You look away for a second and they're gone, and your body just gets all hot. And so I had a little breakdown. Shut the doors! I've lost my daughter! I look around

Halle Berry shopping with daughter Nahla in Los Angeles. Nahla was the subject of a bitter custody battle between Berry and ex-boyfriend Gabriel Aubry.

and, sure enough, 30 seconds later, she pokes her head out: "Hi, Mommy." But it made me think: What if she really did get lost? Would she be able to say who she is? So that night, I said, "What's your mommy's name?" And she looked at me like, You idiot. Why are you asking me what your name is? I asked her again: "Nahla? What is Mommy's name?" She thought about it for a second, and finally she said, "Halle Blueberries!" Blueberries are her favorite fruit.

Quuoted by Jonathan Van Meter. "Halle Berry: Halle's Hollywood." *Vogue*, August 20, 2010. www.vogue.com/magazine/article/halles-hollywood.

In 2009, Berry, daughter Nahla, and Gabriel Aubry were spotted playing on the beach in Miami. Soon after, Berry and Aubry were embroiled in a bitter custody battle over Nahla.

The interview was broadcast on *The Oprah Winfrey Show* in an episode that Winfrey devoted to her friend, titled "Halle Berry's Having a Baby." Berry and Aubry had been trying to conceive a child, and they had finally succeeded. Berry's pregnancy was one of the happiest times of her life. That happiness, however, was marred in September 2007 by a racist letter she received in which the author promised to harm her unborn child. Berry then hired security guards for protection. The threat never materialized, and on March 16, 2008, Berry gave birth to Nahla Ariela Aubry at Cedars-Sinai Medical Center in Los Angeles. Berry chose her daughter's names carefully: Nahla is Arabic for "honeybee" and Ariela is Hebrew for "lion for God."

In a magazine interview in February 2009, Berry said that having Nahla had changed her life: "I thought I knew love before, but I've never felt anything like this."[99] Berry also said Nahla's birth had made her feel more committed to Aubry than she had been to the two men she had married. Berry also said the couple would like to have more children.

Another Broken Relationship

Berry once said of Aubry, "He's a good man and cares for me."[100] But only two years after Nahla was born their relationship ended. They quit living together in April 2010 but did not announce the split publicly until May. Berry's publicist sent e-mails to the news media explaining the breakup, and Aubry released his own statement that said, "I am sad to say that Halle and I have decided together to separate at this time."[101] Both said they wanted to maintain a friendly relationship, because it would be best for their daughter.

There were conflicting news reports on why the celebrity couple had split up. Friends of Berry told reporters the actress, who made much more money than Aubry, was tired of supporting him financially while people in other stories claimed Aubry had simply tired of their relationship. In August Berry denied such reports. She said there was no specific reason for the breakup: "It's just that you realize you are not meant to go the distance with everybody. We were meant to bring this amazing little person [Nahla] into the world. And I think that's why we came together."[102] Berry also said she wanted Aubry to remain a part of her daughter's life; in September he even traveled with Berry to South Africa while she was filming the movie *Dark Tide*.

Their relationship began to deteriorate, however, when both began dating other people. Berry began a relationship with

The Negative Side of Celebrity

Because Halle Berry is famous, problems in her personal life, such as her two divorces and her breakup and subsequent custody battle with Gabriel Aubry over their daughter, Nahla, have become public. Berry, like other celebrities, realizes that one price she pays for her profession is a loss of privacy, because the news media is always ready to discuss the most intimate details of her life. In a March 2011 article by Amy DuBois Burnett in *Ebony* magazine, Berry comments on her loss of privacy and how she has learned to deal with it:

> [The] normal everyday experiences that I go through as a woman get heightened to a level where [they are perceived as] not normal. My experiences are probably no different than yours, but mine get written about, so they seem odd in some way, or that I'm twisted in some way. But I'm struggling just like most women to get it right, to find happiness, to find love, to balance motherhood and career. I'm struggling with all those things like everybody else. But I've learned to tune that out, and I really don't care anymore what people have to say about what I do or who I am, or how I do whatever I do. It's my life, it's my business, and I do it how I choose.

Quoted in Amy DuBois Burnett, "On the Very Solid, Fantastically Full Life of Halle Berry." *Ebony*, March 2011, pp. 82–83.

French actor Olivier Martinez, who plays her husband in *Dark Tide*, and Aubry dated a few different women. A bitter custody fight over Nahla began on December 30, 2010, when Aubry filed legal documents seeking joint custody of their daughter. The legal battle angered both of them and became public as the two celebrities traded accusations through the news media. Some stories claimed that Berry did not trust Aubry to care for Nahla and that he had once uttered a racial slur at her while they argued over the child. Aubry claimed he was a loving father who just wanted to be part of Nahla's life and accused Berry of trying to keep him away from his daughter so she could have total control over Nahla.

The anger between the two died down after a few months, but then flared up again at the end of 2011 and continued into 2012. Berry said that her daughter's welfare was her main concern: "Being a mother is probably the most important thing in my life right now. Career is important, but nothing really supersedes my role as a mother. That's the most important thing I'm going to do in this life at this point."[103]

A Return to Work

Even though Berry was concentrating on being a mother, she was not ready to give up acting, and she returned to work eight months after giving birth. Her next film was *Frankie & Alice*. It is based on a true story about a black dancer in the 1970s named Frankie who has an identity disorder. She has two other personalities—those of a seven-year-old child and a Southern white racist. Berry became determined to play Frankie because the role was so interesting and dramatic. Berry and her agent, Vincent Cirrincione, even helped produce the movie, and Berry got to meet the real Frankie. Berry explains why the role intrigued her so much: "I was ignited by the idea of this woman and intrigued and horrified at the same time, and I thought, wow, how does a black woman, a physically black woman, live with an alter personality that thinks she's white and Southern and a racist, like, how does that happen and then how does one live with the turmoil of that."[104]

Berry's performance as the psychologically troubled woman won rave reviews. *Hollywood Reporter* critic Duane Byrge writes, "Berry is spellbinding as Frankie.... [She] switches from hard-drinking, promiscuous lady of the night to a tee-totaling, racist Southern white belle, and, to boot, a genius-level kid."[105] Berry was nominated for but did not win a Golden Globe for her performance. However, Berry did receive the National Association for the Advancement of Colored People Image Award for outstanding actress in a movie.

Berry returned to the screen after Nahla's birth, playing a black dancer with a personality disorder in Frankie & Alice. *Berry's performance earned her the Outstanding Actress award at the NAACP Image Award ceremony.*

When *Frankie & Alice* opened on December 10, 2010, it was the first film starring Berry that had been released in three years. After the third X-Men movie in 2006, Berry had only appeared in two other movies before *Frankie & Alice*, both in 2007—*Perfect Stranger*, a thriller costarring Bruce Willis, and *Things We Lost in the Fire*. Her long layoff was due to her repeated attempts to become pregnant, time spent with her infant daughter, and her nasty breakup with Aubry.

After completing *Frankie & Alice*, Berry did not slow down. She moved on to film *New Year's Eve* and *Dark Tide*, released in late 2011 and 2012 respectively. In September 2011 she began filming *Cloud Atlas*. All three movies continued Berry's desire to have different types of roles, so she would not get bored playing the same kind of character. *New Year's Eve* is a romantic comedy about how several couples and single people celebrate on the eve of the New Year; Berry plays a nurse. In the thriller *Dark Tide*, Berry plays a diver fascinated by great white sharks whose life is changed by a dangerous encounter with one of the deadly creatures. *Cloud Atlas* is based on a novel that spans many centuries. The stellar cast includes Tom Hanks, Hugo Weaving, Susan Sarandon, and Hugh Grant. Berry and the other actors all play multiple roles. One of Berry's roles is Luisa Rey, a reporter who runs into danger when she investigates a nuclear power plant.

A Multiracial Screen Diva

By successfully playing a wide variety of characters, Berry has achieved her goal of being considered an actress and not just a black actress. In her book, *Divas on Screen: Black Women in American Film*, author Mia Mask explains how black actresses have always struggled for acceptance in an industry dominated by whites. She profiles six actresses, including Dorothy Dandridge, Pam Grier, and Berry. Mask gives them the title of diva because of their importance in shaping the image of black women through their movies. Mask writes that Berry can be considered "a diva of the silver screen because she successfully negotiated the minefield of an industry that has historically closed its doors to people of color. In the multicultural new millennium, she is a celebrity for a multiracial era."[106]

Berry has had an easier time than black actors and actresses of previous generations because of the weakening of racism and a greater social acceptance of blacks that began in the second half of the twentieth century. Berry still, however, had to fight racial stereotyping at times during her career. According to Berry, racism has not entirely disappeared from the film industry: "I'm lucky in that I'm being offered more and more interesting roles that would never have been given to a black woman before. Things have changed a little for colored women, but we still have to fight and though the situation has improved, there's still a long way to go."[107]

Despite having a white mother, Berry has always considered herself African American, because she knows that is how other people identify her. Berry also believes her daughter, Nahla, is black, despite having a white father and a biracial mother. Berry says, however, that when Nahla gets older she will have to answer the question of race for herself: "I had to decide for myself, and that's what she's going to have to decide—how she identifies herself to the world. And I think, largely that will be based on how the world identifies her. [But] I feel like she's black. I'm black and I'm her mother, and I believe in the one-drop theory."[108]

Berry Is Hopeful

Halle Berry's race has shaped both her life and her movie career, and she has shown her allegiance to that racial identity in the film roles she has chosen. Berry believes her biracial daughter, Nahla, will face less racism than she did, and one reason for her optimism was the 2008 election of President Barack Obama, who like Berry had a white mother and black father. Berry attended his inauguration in January 2009, and in an article by Laura Brown in *Harper's Bazaar* magazine, Berry describes the ceremony:

> The inauguration was amazing—being there with people from different races and walks of life. I saw people talking who, before Obama, would never sit down and have a conversation. Nahla will grow up in a completely different America. Obama is someone who's more like her than not, who shares her history. Hopefully she'll grow up in a world where it'll be easier than I had it. I had a rough time. I was accused of stuffing the ballot box for my high school prom-queen election because they couldn't believe the only black girl in the school won.

Quoted in Laura Brown. "Hallelujah." *Harper's Bazaar*, April 8, 2009. http://www.harpersbazaar.com/magazine/cover/halle-berry-0509.

The one-drop theory, first put forth by nineteenth-century Southern racists, states that even the smallest percentage of African American heritage makes a person black. Although Berry long ago came to terms with how people view her racially, it was only as she got older that she was able to become more comfortable in accepting herself for who and what she is.

Halle Berry, seen walking past a photograph of civil rights icon Martin Luther King, Jr., has fought racial stereotyping throughout her career. She was profiled in the book Divas on Screen: Black Women in American Film *because of the triumphs she has achieved in this area.*

A Happy Berry

Berry once said that she went into acting because "I had this real need to be accepted and loved by people. The need for love and acceptance drove me into performing."[109] Berry has freely admitted in the past that this need stemmed from low self-esteem that was caused, at least in part, by being abandoned by her father when she was a child. Berry has also importantly realized that happiness can come from within: "The real trick to finding happiness is to realize it comes from within. I can decide to be happy any day, any moment I want. Nobody controls that any more."[110] It also seems as though Berry may have changed her negative views on marriage as rumors swirled in early 2012 that she was engaged to Oliver Martinez.

If nothing else, Berry's daughter and her long list of accomplishments should keep her happy. She once said in an interview, "I always knew I was going to do something extraordinary because that's the way I grew up, always proving to the world I was good enough."[111] And Berry has definitely done that.

Halle Berry, posing with her star on the Hollywood Walk of Fame, is a Golden Globe winner, an Academy Award winner, and a mother.

Introduction: Actress, History Maker, Barrier Breaker

1. "Hottest in Hollywood." *Ebony*, March 2011, p. 38.
2. Quoted in Amy DuBois Barnett. "On the Very Solid, Fantastically Solid Life of Halle Berry." *Ebony*, March 2011, p. 81.
3. Quoted in Nui Te Koha. "Fireball: The Beatings, the Infidelity, the Suicide Bid, the Oscar. Halle Berry Tells All: Lighting up a Black Journey." *Daily Telegraph* (Sydney), March 28, 2002.
4. Quoted in "Best Actress to Bond Babe: Her Aspirations Are Both Big and Small." *Dallas Morning News*, November 18, 2002.
5. Quoted in Daniel Neman. "Beyond Beauty: Trailblazer Halle Berry Still Exploring Her Own Path." *Richmond (VA) Times-Dispatch*, April 13, 2007.

Chapter 1: Growing up Biracial

6. Quoted in Alina Cho. "Big Stars, Big Giving: Halle Berry on Helping Victims of Domestic Violence." CNN, December 14, 2010. http://am.blogs.cnn.com/2010/12/14/big-stars-big-giving-halle-berry-on-helping-victims-of-domestic-violence.
7. Quoted in John Farley. *Introducing Halle Berry*. New York: Pocket Books, 2002, p. 15.
8. Quoted in Frank Sanello. *Halle Berry: A Stormy Life*. London: Virgin Books, 2004, p. 5.
9. Quoted in "Halle's Hell with Violent Father." *Daily Record* (Glasgow), October 29, 2007.
10. Quoted in Siobhan Synnot. "Berry Happy at Last." *Daily Mirror* (London), April 16, 2007.
11. Quoted in Barbara Davies. "At Last I've Learned to Like Myself." *Daily Mirror* (London), April 18, 2004.
12. Quoted in Synnot. "Berry Happy at Last."
13. Quoted in Farley. *Introducing Halle Berry*, p. 22.

14. Quoted in Karen S. Schneider. "Hurts So Bad." *People*, May 13, 1996. www.people.com/people/archive/article/0,,20141276,00.html.

15. Quoted in Frank Lovece. "Halle Berry Is Poised to Become a Major Star." *Reading (PA) Reader*, July 5, 1992.

16. Quoted in Sanello. *Halle Berry*, p. 12.

17. Quoted in Koha. "Fireball: The Beatings, the Infidelity, the Suicide Bid, the Oscar. Halle Berry Tells All: Lighting up a Black Journey."

18. Quoted in Michelle Tauber. "50 Most Beautiful People." *People*, May 12, 2003. www.people.com/people/archive/article/0,,20140026,00.html.

19. Quoted in "Slave Queen's Search for Love, Acceptance." *Dominion Post* (Morganton, WV), January 6, 1997.

20. Quoted in "Halle Berry's Journey from Miss USA Runner-Up to Oscar Winner." *Access Hollywood*, June 16, 2011. www.accesshollywood.com/halle-berrys-journey-from-miss-usa-runner-up-to-oscar-winner_article_49368.

21. Quoted in Lovece. "Halle Berry Is Poised to Become a Major Star."

22. Quoted in Tim Allis. "The Woman Who Would Be Queen." *People*, February 22, 1993. www.people.com/people/article/0,,20109824,00.html.

23. Quoted in Schneider. "Hurts So Bad."

24. Quoted in Sanello. *Halle Berry*, p. 25.

25. Quoted in Sarah Horrocks. "Halle Berry Interview." sofeminine.co.uk, April 4, 2007. www.sofeminine.co.uk/mag/entertainment/d1441.html.

Chapter 2: Berry Becomes a Movie Actress

26. Quoted in "Halle Berry: From Homeless Shelter to Hollywood Fame." *Reader's Digest*, April 2007, p. 89.

27. Quoted in Schneider. "Hurts So Bad."

28. Quoted in Horrocks. "Halle Berry Interview."

29. Quoted in Bonnie Siegler. "Halle Berry: My Battle with Diabetes." *Daily Mail* (London), December 14, 2005. www.dailymail.co.uk/health/article-371528/Halle-Berry-My-battle-diabetes.html.

30. Quoted in Horrocks. "Halle Berry Interview."
31. Quoted in Siegler. "Halle Berry: My Battle with Diabetes."
32. Quoted in Horrocks. "Halle Berry Interview."
33. Quoted in Terry Keefe. "Halle Berry: The Hollywood Interview." *Venice*, February 2002. http://thehollywoodinterview.blogspot.com/2008/11/halle-berry-hollywood-interview.html.
34. Quoted in Farley. *Introducing Halle Berry*, p. 33.
35. Quoted in Mia Mask. "Halle Berry: The Many Faces of a Diva." NPR, March 5, 2010. www.npr.org/templates/story/story.php?storyId=124330992.
36. Quoted in "When Is a Berry Like a Nut?" *Times* (London), November 21, 2002.
37. Quoted in Sanello. *Halle Berry*, p. 50.
38. Duane Dudek. "Alex Haley's Crowning Finale to his 'Roots.'" *Milwaukee Sentinel*, February 6, 1993.
39. Quoted in Schneider. "Hurts So Bad."
40. Quoted in Farley. *Introducing Halle Berry*, p. 54.
41. Quoted in Allis. "The Woman Who Would Be Queen."
42. Quoted in Schneider. "Hurts So Bad."

Chapter 3: Berry Becomes a Star

43. Quoted in Schneider. "Hurts So Bad."
44. Quoted in Mask. "Halle Berry: The Many Faces of a Diva."
45. Janet Maslin. "A Little Boy and a Plot Worthy of Solomon." *New York Times*, March 17, 1994.
46. Quoted in "Halle Berry Kurt Russell Star in New Action Film 'Executive Decision.'" *Jet*, March 11, 1996, p. 60.
47. Quoted in "Halle Berry Stars in Murder Mystery 'The Rich Man's Wife.'" *Jet*, September 2, 1996, p. 32.
48. Quoted in Sanello. *Halle Berry*, p. 90.
49. Quoted in Allis. "The Woman Who Would Be Queen."
50. Quoted in "Actress Halle Berry and Atlanta Braves' David Justice to Divorce." *Jet*, March 11, 1996, p. 65.
51. Quoted in "Love Strikes Out." *People*, March 11, 1996. www.people.com/people/article/0,,20102991,00.html.
52. Quoted in "David Justice Tells Why He's Divorcing Halle Berry in *Ebony Man* Exclusive." *Jet*, May 26, 1997, p. 60.

53. Quoted in Garth Pearce. "Life's Been One Big Car Crash." *Sunday Times* (London), April 8, 2007.
54. Quoted in Sanello. *Halle Berry*, p. 123.
55. Quoted in "Halle Berry Brings the Passion and Pain of Dorothy Dandridge to HBO Movie." *Jet*, August 23, 1999, p. 6.
56. Quoted in Mia Mask. *Divas on Screen: Black Women in American Film*. Chicago: University of Illinois Press, p. 185.
57. Quoted in Terry Keefe. "With a Landmark Oscar for Her Searing Portrayal of the Gritty Belle of Monster's Ball, Halle Berry's on a Roll." *Venice*, February 2002. http://thehollywoodinterview.blogspot.com/2008/11/halle-berry-hollywood-interview.html.
58. Quoted in Farley. *Introducing Halle Berry*, p. 170.

Chapter 4: Berry Makes Oscar History

59. Quoted in Nick Carter. "'Glitter' Co-Star Reflects on His New Film, Album and Halle Berry." *Milwaukee Journal Sentinel*, September 19, 2001.
60. Quoted in Sanello. *Halle Berry*, p. 127.
61. Quoted in Lancaster. "Halle Berry: Interview," p. 55.
62. Quoted in Mark Dagostino and Paula Yoo. "Collision Course." *People*, April 17, 2000. www.people.com/people/archive/article/0,,20130974,00.html.
63. Quoted in Laura Randolph Lancaster. "Halle Berry: Interview." *Ebony*, August 2000, p. 55.
64. Quoted in Davies. "At Last I've Learned to Like Myself."
65. Quoted in "Halle Berry." *Jet*, September 11, 2000, p. 58.
66. Quoted in Lancaster. "Halle Berry: Interview," p. 55.
67. Quoted in Lancaster. "Halle Berry: Interview," p. 55.
68. Quoted in John Millar. "My Mum Is Xtra Special." *Sunday Mail* (London), May 21, 2006.
69. Quoted in Keefe. "With a Landmark Oscar for Her Searing Portrayal of the Gritty Belle of Monster's Ball, Halle Berry's on a Roll."
70. Quoted in Sanello. *Halle Berry*, p. 155.
71. Quoted in Bruce Kirkland. "Halle Berry Bares Her Soul." *Sun Media*, March 22, 2007. http://jam.canoe.ca/Movies/Artists/B/Berry_Halle/2007/03/22/pf-3804325.html.

72. Quoted in Farley. *Introducing Halle Berry*, p. 199.

73. Quoted in Paul Fischer. "Halle Berry's Monstrous New Role." Film Monthly, December 19, 2001. www.filmmonthly.com/Profiles/Articles/HBerry/HBerry.html.

74. Quoted in Jeffrey M. Anderson. "Interview with Halle Berry: A Berry Good Year." January 17, 2002. www.combustiblecelluloid.com/interviews/halleberry.shtml.

75. Roger Ebert. "Monster's Ball." RogerEbert.com, February 1, 2002. http://rogerebert.suntimes.com/apps/pbcs.dll/article?AID=/20020201/REVIEWS/202010304/1023.

76. Halle Berry. "2002 Oscar Acceptance Address for Best Leading Actress." March 24, 2002.

Chapter 5: Catwoman and Other New Roles

77. Quoted in Fischer. "Halle Berry's Monstrous New Role."

78. Quoted in Phillip McCarthy. "Halle Berry Hasn't Let Oscar Glory—or Catwoman—Stop Her from Starring in Popcorn Thrillers." *Sydney Morning Herald*, April 20, 2007.

79. Quoted in Sanello. *Halle Berry*, p. 213.

80. Quoted in Aldore D. Collier. "Halle Berry Is the Sexy Bond Girl in 'Die Another Day'." *Jet*, November 25, 2002, p. 58.

81. Quoted in Briony Warden. "Bond Saved Me from Choking to Death During Our Love Scene." *The Sun* (London), November 13, 2002.

82. Simon Wheeler. "New 007 Movie Is Best Yet." *The Sun* (London), November 9, 2002.

83. Quoted in "Berry Battles Husband's Sex Addiction." The *Courier Mail* (Brisbane, Australia), November 25, 2002.

84. Quoted in Sanello. *Halle Berry*, p. 233.

85. Quoted in Carter. "'Glitter' Co-Star Reflects on His New Film, Album and Halle Berry."

86. Quoted in Davies. "At Last I've Learned to Like Myself."

87. Quoted in Warden. "Bond Saved Me from Choking to Death During Our Love Scene."

88. John Braithwaite. "Confessions of a Bond Girl." Single Articles. www.singlearticles.com/confessions-of-a-bond-a4815.html.

89. Quoted in Howard Gensler. "Berry Focused: Halle Muses on Career, Beefed-Up Role for Storm in 'X-Men' sequel." *Philadelphia Daily News*, May 24, 2006.

90. Quoted in Ann Hornaday. "'Catwoman': Halle Berry as Claws Celebre." *Washington Post*, July 23, 2004.

91. Quoted in Garth Pearce. "Life's Been One Big Car Crash." *The Sunday Times* (London), April 8, 2007.

92. Quoted in Aldore Collier. "Halle Berry: *Their Eyes Were Watching God*." *Jet*, March 7, 2005.

93. Quoted in Gensler. "Berry Focused."

94. Quoted in Synnot. "Berry Happy at Last."

Chapter 6: A New Starring Role: Motherhood

95. Quoted in McCarthy. "Halle Berry Hasn't Let Oscar Glory—or Catwoman—Stop Her from Starring in Popcorn Thrillers."

96. Quoted in Synnot. "Berry Happy at Last."

97. Claudia Puig. "Del Toro, Berry Anchor 'Things We Lost.'" *USA Today*, October 19, 2007. www.usatoday.com/life/movies/reviews/2007-10-18-things-we-lost_N.htm.

98. Halle Berry. "Halle Berry & Benicio Del Toro." Oprah, October 2, 2007. www.oprah.com/oprahshow/Halle-Berry-and-Benicio-Del-Toro/5#ixzz1Y7Nnb6DM.

99. Quoted in Lesley Messer. "Halle Berry on Her Fierce Love for Her Daughter." *People*, February 9, 2009. www.people.com/people/article/0,,20257585,00.html.

100. Quoted in Jan Janssen. "A Mummy Yes, but a Bride? No Way!" *News of the World*, April 15, 2007, p. 20.

101. Quoted in Cindy Clark. "That Lovin' Feelin' Has Been Lost." *USA Today*, May 3, 2010.

102. Quoted in Jonathan Van Meter. "Halle Berry: Halle's Hollywood." *Vogue*, August 20, 2010. www.vogue.com/magazine/article/halles-hollywood.

103. Quoted in Amy DuBois Burnett. "On the Very Solid, Fantastically Full Life of Halle Berry." *Ebony*, March 2011, p. 85.

104. Quoted in Audi Cornish. "Halle Berry Opens Up About New Role." NPR, December 31, 2010. www.npr.org/2010/12/31/132527850/Halle-Berry-Opens-Up-About-New-Role.

105. Quoted in Duane Byrge. "Frankie & Alice—Film Review." *Hollywood Reporter*, October 14, 2010. www.hollywoodreporter. com/review/frankie-alice-film-review-29595.

106. Mask. *Divas on Screen*, p. 232.

107. Quoted in Horrocks. "Halle Berry Interview."

108. Quoted in Burnett. "On the Very Solid, Fantastically Full Life of Halle Berry," p. 82.

109. Quoted in Farley. *Introducing Halle Berry*, p. 29.

110. Quoted in Barbara Davies and Joanne Hawkins. "Halle Berry: Little girl Lost—and Found." *The Sunday Telegraph* (London), August 10, 2008. www.dailytelegraph.com.au/ lifestyle/sunday-magazine/halle-berry-little-girl-lost-and-found/story-e6frf039-1111117142805.

111. Quoted in Synnot. "Berry Happy at Last."

1966

Halle Berry is born on August 14 in Cleveland, Ohio.

1984

Graduates from Bedford High School in suburban Cleveland.

1985

Wins the Miss Teen All American pageant.

1986

Wins Miss Ohio USA, is second runner-up in the Miss USA contest, and is fifth runner-up in the Miss World pageant.

1989

Gets her first acting role in the television series *Living Dolls*; she is diagnosed with type 1 diabetes.

1991

Makes her movie debut in *Jungle Fever*.

1992

In May Berry is included on *People* magazine's "50 Most Beautiful People" list; on December 31 she marries David Justice.

1996

In April Berry and Justice file for divorce.

2000

Wins several awards, including a Golden Globe Award and an Emmy Award for her role in *Introducing Dorothy Dandridge*.

2001

Marries Eric Benét in January; they separate three years later and divorce in 2005.

2002

On March 24 becomes the first African American to win an Academy Award for Best Actress for her role in *Monster's Ball*.

2005

Begins dating model Gabriel Aubry.

2008

On March 16 gives birth to daughter Nahla Ariela Aubry.

2011

Nominated for the Golden Globe for Best Actress in a Drama for *Frankie & Alice*; begins dating actor Oliver Martinez.

For More Information

Books

John Farley. *Introducing Halle Berry*. New York: Pocket Books, 2002. A solid biography of Halle Berry.

Patricia M. Hinds, ed. *50 of the Most Inspiring African-Americans*. New York: Essence, 2005. Includes a profile of Halle Berry.

Melissa Ewey Johnson. *Halle Berry: A Biography*. Santa Barbara, CA: Greenwood, 2010. A fact-filled biography about Halle Berry.

Frank Sanello. *Halle Berry: A Stormy Life*. London: Virgin Books, 2004. One of the best biographies about Halle Berry.

Michael Schuman. *Halle Berry: "Beauty Is not Just Beautiful."* Berkeley Heights, NJ: Enslow, 2006.

Periodicals

Amy DuBois Barnett. "On the Very Solid, Fantastically Solid Life of Halle Berry." *Ebony*, March 2011. Halle Berry talks about her daughter, Nahla, and her life in this in-depth interview.

Nui Te Koha. "Fireball: The Beatings, the Infidelity, the Suicide Bid, the Oscar. Halle Berry Tells All: Lighting up a Black Journey." *Daily Telegraph* (Sydney), March 28, 2002. This article details Halle Berry's life.

Internet Sources

"Halle Berry & Benicio Del Toro." Oprah, October 2, 2007. http://www.oprah.com/oprahshow/Halle-Berry-and-Benicio-Del-Toro/5#ixzz1Y7Nnb6DM. Berry discusses why she wanted to become a mother and other aspects of her life.

"Halle Berry's Acceptance Speech." March 2002. Blackfilm.com. http://blackfilm.com/20020326/features/a-halleberryacceptance.shtml. Berry's emotional speech on accepting the Oscar for *Monster's Ball*.

Laura Brown. "Hallelujah." *Harper's Bazaar*, April 8, 2009. http://www.harpersbazaar.com/magazine/cover/halle-berry-0509. Berry talks about the joy of being a mother.

Barbara Davies and Joanne Hawkins. "Halle Berry: Little Girl Lost—and Found." *The Sunday Telegraph* (London), August 10, 2008. http://www.dailytelegraph.com.au/lifestyle/sunday-magazine/halle-berry-little-girl-lost-and-found/story-e6frf039-1111117142805. A lot of information about Berry's early life.

Karen S. Schneider. "Hurts So Bad." *People*, May 13, 1996. http://www.people.com/people/archive/article/0,,20141276,00.html. Berry discusses her divorce from David Justice and her early life.

Bonnie Siegler. "Halle Berry: My Battle with Diabetes." *Daily Mail* (London), December 14, 2005. http://www.dailymail.co.uk/health/article-371528/Halle-Berry-My-battle-diabetes.html. Berry discusses in detail what it is like to have diabetes.

Websites

IMDb: Halle Berry (http://www.imdb.com/name/nm0000932/). This site has information on Halle Berry's movies and life and links to biographies and other sites about her.

People: Halle Berry. (http://www.people.com/people/halle_berry/0,,,00.html). This is the website for *People* magazine. It offers a biography, photographs, videos, and other information about Halle Berry, including *People* magazine articles about her.

Picture Credits

Cover: © Allstar Picture Library/Alamy

© 20th Century Fox/Marvel Entertainment Group/The Kobal Collection/Art Resource, NY, 57

© Allstar Picture Library/Alamy, 84

© Amblin/Universal/The Kobal Collection/Art Resource, NY, 33

© AP Images/Dave Caulkin, 21

© AP Images/Matt Sayles, 77

© Bettmann/Corbis, 48

© CBS Photo Archive/Getty Images, 34

© Christinne Muschi/Reuters/Landov, 69

© David Aguilera/BuzzFoto/FilmMagic/Getty Images, 80

© Dreamworks/The Kobal Collection/Doane Gregory/Art Resource, NY, 78

© Esparza/Katz Prod/The Kobal Collection/Baldwin, Sidney/Art Resource, NY, 47

© Fred Prouser/Reuters/Landov, 58

© George De Sota/Newsmakers/Getty Images, 42

© Getty Images, 62

© Jeanne Baptise Lacroix/Wire Image/Getty Images, NY, 79

© Kevin Mazur/WireImage/Getty Images, 50

© Kevin Winter/Getty Images, 28, 52

© Kurt Krieger/Corbis, 9

© L.Cohen/WireImage/Getty Images, 74

© LionsGate/The Kobal Collection/Jeanne Louise Bulliard/Art Resource, NY, 60

© Mark Davis/Getty Images, 14

© MGM/EON/The Kobal Collection/Hamshere, Keith/Art Resource, NY, 66

© Mike Carrillo/Getty Images, 53

© Paramount/The Kobal Colletion Art Resource, NY, 39

© Presselect/Alamy, 15, 87, 88

© Ronald C. Modra/Sports Imagery/Getty Images, 36

© SGranitz/WireImage/Getty Images, 63

© Universal/The Kobal Collection/David Lee/Art Resource, NY, 31

© Warner Bros./DC Comics/The Kobal Collection/Art Resource, NY, 73

© Warner Bros/ABC-TV/The Kobal Collection/Art Resource, NY, 27

Michael V. Uschan has written more than eighty books, including *Life of an American Soldier in Iraq*, for which he won the 2005 Council for Wisconsin Writers Juvenile Nonfiction Award. Uschan began his career as a writer and editor with United Press International, a wire service that provided stories to newspapers, radio, and television. Uschan considers writing history books a natural extension of the skills he developed in his many years as a journalist. He and his wife, Barbara, reside in the Milwaukee suburb of Franklin, Wisconsin.